Stopping Places

A Gypsy History of South London and Kent

SIMON EVANS

UNIVERSITY OF HERTFORDSHIRE PRESS

First published in Great Britain in 2004 by
University of Hertfordshire Press
Learning and Information Services
University of Hertfordshire
College Lane
Hatfield
Hertfordshire AL10 9AB

Reprinted in 2008

British Library Cataloguing in Publication Data
A catalogue record for this book is available from the British Library

ISBN 978-1-902806-30-3

Design by Geoff Green, Cambridge, CB4 5RA
Cover design by John Robertshaw, Harpenden, AL5 2JB
Printed in Great Britain by Antony Rowe Ltd, Chippenham, SN14 6LH

Contents

———

Acknowledgements

———

M ost of the research that had to be undertaken to write this book was funded by the Bromley Gypsy Traveller Project based in St Mary Cray in Kent. It has been estimated that the area has one of the highest Gypsy Traveller populations in the UK for reasons that will become apparent to readers of this book.

For the thirty years that the organisation has been in existence it has assisted thousands of Travellers, whether on the roadside, housed or on sites, in their dealings with the institutions of sedentary society. This work has consisted mainly of providing practical support and skills in areas such as education, housing and local authority provision.

Many of the difficulties that Travellers face in their day-to-day inter-actions with the Gorjer are the result of prejudice and misunderstanding and so it was decided that it was important to tell the story of this signif-icant section of the local community. This book is the result of that deci-sion and without the support of the Bromley Gypsy Traveller project it would probably never have been written.

I am also grateful to all those Travellers who willingly gave up their time to ply me with cups of tea and patiently relate their family history to me. Also to all those who generously allowed me to copy precious personal photographs for inclusion in this book. I hope I have done them all justice.

List of Illustrations

―――――

p148 Delaine and Damien leBas SE
p149 Cherry picking, Pembury, 1992 SE
p150 On Polhill, 1988 SE
p152 Pembury, 1992 SE
p154 Sandwich bar, Biggin Hill, 2001 SE
p155 Sussex lay by, 1989 SE
p156 Mark Hilden cherry picking, 1987 SE
p157 Pub in Medway Towns, 2001 SE
p158 Sarah SE
p160 Derby Day, Epsom, 1988 SE
p162 Mrs Smith, Maidstone SE
p163 Reuben and his family, Green St Green SE
p164 Mushi SE
p166 On Polhill SE

LEGEND

BAK	Baker family
BERK	Berkley family
BEX	Bexleyheath Local Studies
BRA	Brazil family
BROM	Bromley Local Studies
BUT	Butler family
CKS	Centre for Kentish Studies
EM	Epsom Museum
GRE	Greenwich Heritage Centre
KM	Kent Messenger
KTN	Kentish Times Newspapers
LIV	University of Liverpool
LUK	The Luke Family
MAJ	Alan Major
MED	Medway Local Studies
MERT	Merton Local Studies
SE	Simon Evans
SEV	Sevenoaks Local Studies
TOP	Topham Picturepoint
UK	Unknown

Introduction

————

Now that the sight of brightly painted horse-drawn wagons on the road is just a distant memory and the travelling life has all but disappeared, many people conclude that the Gypsies themselves have also disappeared. Those who follow this line of reasoning seem not to wonder where the Gypsies may actually have gone and what has happened to the grandsons and granddaughters of those who once travelled the highways and byways.

Today, the presence of a group of modern caravans on some patch of waste ground or on a council site frequently provokes the opinion that the occupants cannot possibly be 'real Gypsies'. The implication is that the 'true Romany' of the past was a trustworthy and valued person, but that these people who live in motor-drawn trailers and don't play fiddles around camp fires at night are mere pretenders, just 'didikais' and dirty 'pikies'. The real Gypsies of old, it is argued, were of pure Romany blood; their ancestors belonged to a tribe of musicians

Leaving Epsom downs after the Derby, 1938

1

Although these 19th century etchings were an accurate portrayal, they still tended to romanticise Gypsy life

and dancers who left India about a thousand years ago. They were a mysterious people who lived in gaily painted horse-drawn caravans and gazed into crystal balls, but apart from the occasional fortune-teller in a booth at the seaside they have died out – all gone.

This false analysis is a ploy which is frequently used to deny that today's Travellers have a culture and history of their own. Once robbed of their identity, they can then be dismissed as mere vagrants, itinerants and scoundrels – anything but 'proper' Gypsies. Yet, in common with the rest of humanity, there never have been any racially or culturally 'pure' Gypsies. All races of people have evolved over the centuries; cultures are a blend of nationalities and global influences, the product of invasion, immigration and colonisation, of trade, travel and communication. The English Gypsies are no different from anyone else in this respect: contemporary Traveller culture is the product of generations of influence and interaction.

This notion of the 'real Gypsy' or the 'pure Romany' became popular amongst nineteenth-century romantic folklorists who studied the ways of the Travellers through the microscope of the new science of anthropology. During the expansion of the Victorian Empire, new races were being discovered on vast foreign continents, but here at home in England was an exotic, tribal culture on their very doorstep. Gypsies were an ideal subject for these amateur enthusiasts who didn't have to travel very far to take a step into an unknown and mysterious world in order to study and theorise about those who inhabited it. These

An Elizabethan beggar

An Elizabethan peddlar

'Gypsiologists' adopted the methods and attitudes of the newly fashionable anthropologists working in far-flung corners of the Empire and applied them to this indigenous, but apparently foreign, culture. They observed the customs, language, beliefs and lifestyles of the Gypsies and documented their traditions of song, music and storytelling. Interest grew and by 1888 there were enough of these enthusiasts with funds of material to share for the Gypsy Lore Society to come into being.

Londoners on a Kent hop farm, their open cart has been transformed
into a makeshift caravan

It was observed that some Gypsy families were darker and
more foreign in appearance than others and the conclusion was
made that these people must be the most racially pure and genuine, untainted by contact with the outside world. Those dark
Gypsies who lived in the wildest and most remote regions and
apparently hadn't diluted their blood through intermarriage
with the Gorjer (non-Gypsies) were therefore considered to be
the best subjects to document and study.

This quest for authenticity and a singular ancestral origin
was founded on theories that had been developed by eigh-
teenth-century scholars who studied the Romany language
and found that it had much in common with a Sanskrit
dialect spoken in the Indus valley in the ninth century. Further

Washday outside the hoppers' huts at East Farleigh near Maidstone. It was an outdoor existence as the huts themselves were only large enough for sleeping in. Faggots of firewood were provided by the farmer for the cooking fires

linguistic analysis and a study of ancient Persian legend produced a widely accepted theory that a tribe of people left India about eleven hundred years ago. The ensuing diaspora flowed through Persia and into eastern Europe between 1000 and 1300 AD, then on through western Europe and into the British Isles a couple of hundred years later. Although there are several theories, no one knows for certain why this particular group of people should have left their homeland nor whether they did so voluntarily.

Having established the Asian origins of the language, the Gypsiologists then assumed that those people who were darkest and spoke most Romany were the most 'authentic' Gyspies. They were obviously closest to their ethnic origins, the thoroughbreds with the best pedigree, and therefore top of the Gypsy hierarchy and deserving of most respect. Conversely, this also inevitably meant that those who were less dark, knew less Romany and lived in urban areas were not quite the real thing; their bloodlines were corrupted and they lacked racial purity. Today's Travellers still suffer the legacy of this misguided

Travellers on Mitcham common during fair week 1900

analysis and whenever a local newspaper reports an 'invasion' of Gypsies there will inevitably be correspondence the following week from readers denouncing them as 'not real Gypsies'.

However, if it was through linguistic analysis that the Asian component of Gypsy culture was first identified, then we should look more closely at the language of the contemporary Traveller, because further examination reveals clues to other historical ingredients in the mix. The Romany language or *Romanes* that is currently spoken is more complex than a mere mixture of some ancient Indian words mixed with English and other borrowings picked up on the long journey across Europe.

It was in 1505 that the presence of 'Egiptianis' was first recorded in Scotland, but they do not appear in English documents until 1514 when a witness at an inquest was described as an 'Egypcyan' woman who apparently had considerable skill at palm reading. Over subsequent decades there are increasing references to bands of dark-skinned and exotically dressed people travelling on horseback throughout the length of Britain.

They were generally viewed with suspicion, along with anyone else who appeared not to belong to any particular place, including the likes of the 'sturdy beggars' of Elizabethan England. These were popularly considered to be an able-bodied and quick-thinking class of people who, rather than begging, should have been earning an honest wage. They were the 'undeserving poor', a mixed bunch of vagrants, discharged retainers and ex-soldiers, bands of unemployed, masterless men and ex-servants. Having no fixed abode, they slept in barns and outhouses or else inhabited common lodging houses. Unlike those who were forced into life on the streets through physical or mental disability, they were perceived as workshy and unworthy of charity. These vagabonds lived on

Charcoal burner's camp

their wits outside the law and spoke their own dialect, or *cant*, in order to communicate secretly with each other. Any nomadic people arriving in the British Isles would inevitably have had some interaction with others who also lived on the roads, outside the conventions of sedentary society. Some words of Elizabethan *cant* – for example *ken* for 'house', *jigger* for 'door' and *mort* for a woman – still remain in the vocabulary of today's Travellers.

Also present in the contemporary Traveller lexicon are words from East London rhyming slang, another mode of speech used specifically to enable communication within a culture but to confuse the outsider. The Cockney, the wheeler-dealer, the barrow boy, the rag and bone man with his horse and trolley also have a measure of cultural affinity with the Traveller. Although the 'East Ender' may not be an itinerant, attitudes towards money, property, community, family and authority find parallels in the Gypsy outlook. In Kent, the East Enders and Travellers spent a month every year working and living alongside each other in the hop gardens. The Cockneys learnt about the outdoor Gypsy life, cooking on open fires and living simply in huts, barns or cowsheds; the Travellers got to know something of working-class inner-city ways from these unpretentious Gorjers.

Other nomadic people included labourers working on large civil-engineering projects who became known as navigators or 'navvies' during the great boom of canal-building in the eighteenth century. They simply followed the work, moving from one construction project to another and living in camps, often with their families. Later, this mobile workforce dug railway

A charcoal burner, West Kent

cuttings and tunnels and built embankments, viaducts, roads and eventually motorways. Scottish and Irish Travellers also travelled through Kent looking for casual work, particularly during hop picking, the Irish with their own language *Shelta*. Show people, circus and fairground families also bring their own culture into the mix, separate from the Gypsies but still living a Travelling life in the summer and stopping in permanent yards over winter. Although the formal, ring-based circus as we know it wasn't created until the late eighteenth century, it drew upon an older tradition of travelling entertainment. Before the days of mechanical rides, travelling fairs had a wide range of entertainment and attractions, particularly dramatic and musical. The language that evolved within this travelling community of players and showmen came to be known as *Parlary* and its components are as diverse as the people who created it. Much of it is Italian, probably brought by the large number of Italian performers, puppeteers and clowns who came to work here in the early nineteenth century.

Words of cant, Romany and London slang all figure prominently in Parlary; contemporary Shelta also contains some Romany words although it is predominantly comprised of ancient Gaelic, as is the highland Scots Traveller language, the

Evening meal time for pea pickers c. 1890. There was ample temporary work on the county's farms to support a substantial itinerant work force

Beurla Reagaird. This linguistic mix within the various Traveller languages could only have been created by interaction between the different communities.

There have always been people who make their living on the move and do not form part of a permanent, fixed community. Until the industrial revolution, the densely forested Weald of Kent and Sussex was the centre of the nation's iron smelting, casting and forging industries. The rich red clays were high in iron ore and, before the advent of the blast furnace which took the work away to the northern coalfields, charcoal was the fuel used for firing the smelting process. Charcoal was also used for firing oast kilns as well as being a raw ingredient in the manufacture of gunpowder in various locations along the north Kent coast. Although considerable amounts of charcoal were needed, it was made in small-scale clamps and retorts by mobile families who lived in the woods, moving to a new clearing each season. In addition, the county's extensive paper-making industry required considerable quantities of timber for pulp, the trees being coppiced in rotation to produce a sustainable crop. There were also many other woodland products which were made in situ including spile fencing, sheep hurdles and chair parts. The craftsmen who made them all followed their work in the same way as the charcoal burners and coppice workers, living in makeshift huts and camps in a different wood each year, following a cycle of timber harvesting.

Tent-dwelling hop pickers, Kent 1870

In previous centuries, many farm labourers were also semi-itinerant, contracts were frequently only for a year at a time and they moved from farm to farm living in tied accommodation, the younger men often sleeping in sheds or outhouses and the women in the farmhouse lofts. They owned very little and remained in this insecure lifestyle until settling down, marrying and hopefully finding a permanent post with a tied cottage. Even then they had no security of tenure: any job with tied accommodation could still be terminated on the spot and families evicted almost instantaneously. In comparison to those workers in skilled trades and other professions higher in the social pecking order, who had a greater degree of self-determination, this labouring class were closer to the Traveller in lifestyle and outlook. They owned little and relied on family bonds for security; they were never in a position of authority over others and were always at risk of an enforced move.

During the eighteenth century there were also considerable numbers of travelling men who had been discharged from the armed services and for one reason or another were unable to settle down in one place. They may well have become institutionalised, having been clothed, fed and accommodated for much of their lives and, when no longer of use as fighting men through injury or old age, simply abandoned. Richard Wilson, who was examined as a vagrant in 1740, had been a 'beggar and vagabond' since leaving the Navy fourteen years previously.

In 1777, sixty-two-year-old John Webb said that he had been discharged wounded from the army after thirty years' service and now travelled about the country as a stick maker.

There have always been people who have drifted in and out of houses at different times of their lives or during different seasons of the year. An itinerant way of life was the norm for hawkers, travelling craftsmen and journeymen with particular skills, be they stonemasons, basket makers, potters, blacksmiths, pan and kettle menders or hop pickers. These people were not part of some 'underclass' that existed beneath the artisan worker, but they belonged to a fluid social layer without clear boundaries. Although there has always been a degree of antagonism, pride or self-determination separating these loosely definable groups of Gypsies, Travellers, showmen, itinerant workers and other 'outsiders', it is also true that they share a lot of cultural common ground. That the Asian element of Romany culture plays a major part in defining contemporary Traveller identity in Kent is without doubt, but it is only one component in a much more complex mix.

We can get into all the stuff about Indian origins but we have to be quite clear and logical when we talk about Travellers. What is the likelihood that this group of people are going to be the direct descendants of an Asiatic swarthy group of people? I have doubts about that single line of lineage when what we are really looking at is a kind of cacophony of different cultures.

When I look around me I see groups like the drovers in Wales, the people who would drive the cattle down from the northern farms into places like Cardiff where the main droves would be taken to London and after a time the cattle trains would take them to London. This trade gradually disappears with the industrialisation of farms but you leave a group of people who have found an alternative way of making a living on the move. The same thing goes for the fen people in East Anglia, the northern weavers who followed the shearing up the country from the Midlands to the border area and in Kent the same kind of thing would apply.

If you just look at farming, what it requires is a large mobile workforce, still local to certain areas with certain recognised skills that change over time.

Brian Belton

CHAPTER ONE

The Old Ways

——

K ent is affectionately known as the Garden of England. Not
just because it has a homely, rolling landscape with small,
neat fields bordered by well-tended hedgerows, but because
historically the county was charged with the task of feeding
London – thus it was also the Market Garden of England. Apart
from the introduction of steam during the late seventeenth and
early eighteenth century to power the threshing machines and
enable a limited amount of mechanised ploughing, farming
methods had changed little for centuries until the first tractors
arrived in the 1930s. Arable agriculture is labour intensive:

The Smith family near Sevenoaks

ploughing and cultivation relied on horse power, as did sowing, but harvesting, thinning and a certain amount of weeding could only be done by hand. The regular round of seasonal work kept the local workforce busy, but as soon as each crop ripened it needed to be gathered in quickly. Hops had been introduced to Kent during the sixteenth century and although they were not immediately acceptable to many as a flavouring and preservative in beer, by 1724 there were 6,000 acres of hop gardens in East Kent alone. It is not just at picking time that hop growers require extra labour. Apart from the normal care and cultivation that any crop requires, hops need special attention. Unlike other climbers, they do not naturally find their way up the strings and the new shoots have to be 'trained' or 'twiddled' to encourage them to climb. At the same time, surplus shoots have to be cut out, a considerable task that has to be undertaken within a comparatively short period. Traditionally, hop training was the first job of the year to require an additional work force, in the spring when there was much else to be done on the farm, keeping the locals busy.

The Smith family picking strawberries

The county of Kent was also famous for its cherries that ripened during the hot midsummer months, together with soft fruit including strawberries, blackcurrants and gooseberries. Vegetables also needed harvesting, and although brassicas could be cut over a longer period, picking crops like peas and beans was labour intensive. Plums and damsons were ready in late summer and the hops needed picking in early September. As each of these crops ripened in succession they had to be quickly harvested in order to be sent to market in peak condition. Although it is well known that East Enders from London came in their droves for the annual hopping, at the end of the last century they represented only a third of the 250,000 strong workforce that arrived in the county to pick the hops. Apart from the 'home dwellers', most of the rest were itinerants and Travellers from as far afield as Ireland. After hopping, the top fruit was ripening and attention turned to the apple and pear orchards, after which the packing sheds needed to be manned. East Kent and Romney Marsh grew vegetables, particularly

Pulled up on a hop farm

potatoes, which were ploughed up in preparation for the back-breaking task of being picked up by hand in early winter.

Kent's rural economy depended on its mobile workforce, hanging on at one farm after each crop was harvested before moving on in preparation for the next seasonal task. It was a regular cycle that had existed for generations and today many Travellers still work for farmers whose grandfathers employed their grandfathers.

> *When the spring come we'd come up and do the hop training. We used to dress them first, used to have the hoes and knock them out, you know, and cut them off. Then we used to hang on until the hop training. After we'd done the hop training we'd just run up the Derby and then we'd come back and go cherry picking. We used to go from one job to another, do the summer's work right through and then we'd get to the hopping. After that we'd got a job of apple picking and then when they'd finished, about November or something, we used to go potato picking-up, we used to pick them up a shilling a bag. Then after that we used to travel round for the winter again, making swag and that. We used to make a few clothes pegs, get a bob here and there, get a bit of hedge cutting from the farmers. We used to do that until the time came round again for the same thing.*
>
> Jim Harris

Although nomadic in lifestyle, the Travellers did not follow a random route, neither did they necessarily cover very large distances. It was better to stay within an area in which you knew the roads, the good and the bad employers, the local farmers

On a hop farm near Maidstone, 1890

and the stopping places. When Elizabeth Ellison was examined by magistrates in 1794 on suspicion of being a vagrant, she said that she had been born in Ightham, 'since which time she hath travelled about the country without settled habitation in a state of vagrancy but for the last ten years hath travelled and lived in various parts of Kent, Surrey and Essex occasionally with one William Ellison by whom she hath had four children all born in a state of bastardy in the parishes of Otford, Wickham, Ightham and Coulsdon, Surrey.'

William Brazill and his wife Ann had a son John baptised at Penshurst in 1768 where they had lived for about thirty-five years. John was apprehended as a vagrant at Edenbridge in 1806 and again at Rotherfield, Sussex, with his mother, wife and family later in the same year. His brother or perhaps son, was born in the Isle of Oxney and was in his turn apprehended as a vagrant at Rotherfield with his wife and child and again two years later at Wrotham. The Brazill family had thus continued travelling over several generations, but again within a fairly small area. There are many records of vagrants brought in for questioning who were clearly from families who had always travelled, either as labourers or plying trades suited to travelling (including chimney sweeps, chair bottomers, stick cutters, razor grinders and peddlers).

Parish records show that in the nineteenth century Gypsies regularly camped in the same places, many towns and cities

Near Shoreham, Kent

having an area on their outskirts or in some rundown neighbourhood where they would be tolerated. Between 1825 and
1838 there were encampments in the parishes of Chilham, Old
Wives Lees, Godmersham Hill and White Hill. At Seasalter in
1835 the local constable removed four tents of Gypsies on 27
October, three tents from Foxes Cross Lane on 30 November
and three carts full on 21 December. Parish records of baptisms
and deaths also indicate regular stops. The register of the parish
of St Martin in Canterbury has a number of entries between
1822 and 1838 which refer to the presence of Travellers,
including 'children of travellers', 'a hawker' and 'a travelling
brazier' whose abode was Fordwich Lane. From their occupa-
tions and their surnames (Gypsy family names such as Lee,
Scamp and Barton) it is obvious that they were mainly Gypsies.
Some of the families at Fordwich Lane had children baptised in
different years, clearly indicating that it was a place to which
they regularly returned. In September 1791 a party of Lees and

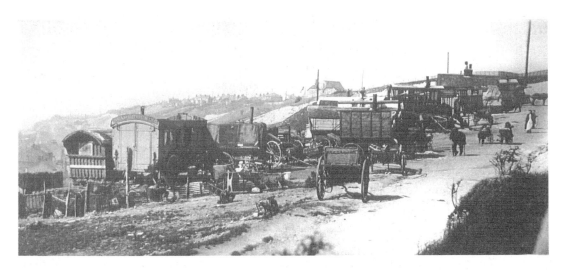

Ash Tree Lane in Chatham had been a stopping place since the nine-teenth century. This picture was probably taken about 1920

Coopers had been taken as vagrants in Chatham after leaving their home in Windsor to 'come into the country to hop picking and harvesting'.

The recorded birthplaces of Travellers and their offspring in the 1881 census confirms that most didn't stray too far from the area with which they were familiar. Kent's neighbouring counties of Essex and Surrey also had very high Traveller populations and were part of the local Gypsy 'map'. Of the 230 Travellers living on Mitcham common in Surrey in 1881 almost a quarter gave Kent as their birthplace. Surrey had very similar crops to Kent, with the same requirement for seasonal labour, but its northernmost corner included the large commons at Mitcham, Wimbledon, Wandsworth and Putney Heath. These were very close to central London and provided ideal stopping places, whilst the surrounding area was still rural farmland dotted with small towns and villages. There was plenty of work, particularly on the herb and lavender farms for which the locality was famous. Lavender and watercress were hawked around the area and many of the street sellers of lavender in central London were Gypsies who bought their supplies directly from the growers in Mitcham.

The open heathland of the North Downs also

Mrs Sparrohawk selling lavender in Mitcham

Harvesting lavender in Mitcham

Epsom Downs, 1938

provided stopping places, particularly around Epsom where the
Derby took place. This annual event had grown from a single
race in 1780 to a much larger event with a fair. Most rural
towns and villages had at least one annual fair day and the fairs
at Epsom racecourse during the Derby and on Mitcham

Greenwich 1880s. The grinding barrow was a complete mobile work-shop. Tin is being cut, probably to repair a pot; there is also an umbrella awaiting repair and what appears to be a burner on the top, presumably to heat a soldering iron

A hawker with rabbits, Greenwich 1880s

A family of basket sellers at Halstead near Sevenoaks in the early twentieth century. They have a 'brush wagon' which was favoured by hawkers
because it afforded extra storage space for their wares

common were an added attraction for Travellers. The fairs were
an important part of the Travelling economy because, in addition to the annual round of agricultural work, many Travellers
also made a living as itinerant salesmen. In the 1881 census
most Travellers and Gypsies in Kent were described as peddlars,
hawkers or general dealers although others were described as
cutlers, basket makers, skewer makers and tinkers.

Fairs were originally incorporated by Royal Charter in
medieval times. Horses and other stock animals were driven to
town to be sold and stallholders set out their wares. They were
not just farmers but included all manner of travelling salesmen
and merchants dealing in household items as well as fancy
goods, trinkets, toys and finery. People from the surrounding
areas would converge on the town for the duration of the fair,
which could sometimes last for several days. It was a special
occasion, a day out in town, when people would meet up with
neighbours and friends and spend as much time socialising

Basket seller in The Avenue, Bexleyheath

and catching up on gossip as on serious business. Inevitably they also provided an opportunity for travelling performers – jugglers, minstrels and acrobats – to provide entertainment for the crowds. As time went on, plays were performed in booths by travelling actors; there were performing animals, freak shows, clowns and musicians. Games of skill and participation were popular as were dance booths and prizefighting, sports such as running races and horse racing, wrestling and cock-fighting. By the nineteenth century the country fairs had become a mixture of market and carnival, a time of licence when people would let their hair down and have a good day out.

Sevenoaks, a sizeable market town, held two annual fairs, one on 29 June and another on the feast of St Nicholas on 6 December. After the Reformation these two fair days were combined into a single two-day event which took place in the High Street on 12 and 13 October. The Victorian middle classes disapproved of the riotous and high-spirited pastimes of the lower orders and between 1868 and 1874 there were several attacks

Fair day on Westerham Green

on the right to hold fairs. In 1871 Parliament passed the Fairs
Act which provided a legal basis for ending them; it stated that
they 'are unnecessary, are the cause of grievous immorality and
are very injurious to the inhabitants of the towns where the
fairs are held'. By this time the high streets in which most fairs
were held had become dominated by shops and small businesses and the last thing these local traders wanted was to have
their main thoroughfare blocked with commercial rivals.
Sevenoaks was just one of many country fairs which succumbed under the new legislation.

It wasn't only the new Act that was to affect the nation's
fairs. New technology in the form of steam power was also
about to bring about a profound change. Until 1865, when the
first steam-driven roundabout appeared, rides and roundabouts
were small and manually operated by a handle. In subsequent
decades steam power allowed mechanical rides to become

Travellers with a dancing bear being seen on their way by the police after Derby week. Epsom, c. 1910

increasingly sophisticated to the extent that they began to displace the other forms of entertainment and trade on the fairground. Eventually they were so popular that they dominated the fairs. Until this time the distinctions between showmen and salesmen, between the spieler outside the booth or freakshow and the travelling hawkers and peddlars who plied their trade alongside them were minimal. Quick to recognise an opportunity, the ride-owning showmen swiftly modernised. The horse-drawn booths, stalls and living wagons gave way to large, highly engineered rides and ornate living trailers, all towed by steam traction engines. Within a few decades the old country fairs had become a thing of the past as the new laws which favoured the sedentary trader over his travelling counterpart took effect.

Using legislation to discourage mobility was nothing new. Governments had been using the law to control the movement and activities of travelling people for centuries. Even by the thirteenth century the open roads had long been considered unsafe and populated with dangerous people; these outsiders lived in taverns with no apparent means of support and so were

Sevenoaks Fair in the nineteenth century

assumed to be up to no good. In 1285 the Statute of Windsor sought to regularise Anglo-Saxon legislation to keep the roads safe and towns secure from strangers. Amongst other measures, the gates were ordered to be closed from sunset to sunrise and watches were to be kept during the night, with bailiffs required to make enquiries about any strangers within the walls.

However, it may not only have been the physical security of the population that was at stake. Anyone who didn't participate in sedentary society posed a challenge to the controlled and governed system: mobility has always been seen as a threat to those who have a vested interest in the stability and order of the status quo. When hawkers, travelling players or musicians arrived in a village or town they brought with them more than mere material goods, they also peddled stories of distant places and knowledge of life elsewhere. They were part of a mobile community who brought news and gossip which they shared and embellished over jugs of ale at wayside inns after a day on the road. It was an itinerant culture that challenged the igno-rance of those who were tied to the land – their knowledge of the outside world could undermine the fixed order of the sedentary community.

Inevitably there were many peasants who sought to loosen themselves from the bonds that tied them to their local landowners, especially if they were kept in a state of perpetual poverty by low wages. Those that survived the Black Death were

Mitcham Fair, 1910

assisted in this aspiration by the fact they were now part of a seriously reduced population and were offering their labour in a seller's market. This desire to travel and its attendant social disruption was obviously not in the interests of landowners, and in 1372 it was noted in Parliament that 'labourers and servants flee from one county to another, some into strange districts to work, on account of the excessive wages, none remaining for certain in any place'. In 1376 the Commons of the Good Parliament confirmed previous statutes and prohibitions against going out of a man's 'own district'. If someone ran away, they were deemed to be outside the law and it was not always possible to settle again without first having to face punishment. It was assumed that those who did escape to travel the roads would have no visible means of supporting themselves other than begging or crime:

> wandering labourers become mere beggars in order to lead an idle life, and betake themselves out of their district commonly to the cities, boroughs and other towns to beg, and they are able bodied and might well ease the community if they would serve.

25

An itinerant piper
playing outside an inn

A travelling metal
worker carrying his
tools and bellows on
his back being seen off
by a dog

Any Gypsies who didn't leave the country
when requested could be executed under
the 1562 Act

(above) Gypsy children being carried in baskets, and
(below) being carried on horseback

In 1383, in order to dissuade people from taking up the wandering life, Justices of the Peace were required to examine vagabonds and bind them to good behaviour or commit them to prison. Five years later vagrancy was forbidden, all 'beggars impotent to serve' were to remain where they were or be sent back to their place of birth whilst beggars able to work were to be set in the stocks.

Further legislation against vagrancy followed and the first measure specifically aimed at Gypsy Travellers was enacted in 1530 with 'an Act concerning outlandish people, calling themselves Egyptians'. Accused of fortune-telling, deception, felony and robbery, 'Egyptians' had to leave England within forty days after this commandment or be imprisoned and forfeit their goods.

An Elizabethan hawker or 'swingman'

Travelling people were perceived as a threat to the settled population. Being strangers, they were not to be trusted, they had no allegiance to the communities they passed through and they were suspected of being petty thieves and tricksters. Destitute vagrants unable to work were a burden on parish finances, unlike mobile tradesmen who were self-sufficient and not dependent on charity. In recognition of this, an exception was made in 1552 whereby, 'Tinkers, pedlars, petty chapmen and "such-like vagrant persons" were to be licensed by two or three Justices of the Peace on pain of fourteen days' imprisonment'. During the reign of Elizabeth I, laws became increasingly punitive: vagrants were to be whipped before being sent back to their own parishes, or in certain circumstances banished overseas. In 1562 an act 'For further punishment of Vagabonds calling themselves Egyptians' became law. All persons of their company, whether foreigners or English-born, except children under the age of fourteen years, were liable to be treated as guilty of felony, leading to the death penalty and forfeiture of goods.

Thomas Harman, a rural Kentish magistrate who took a special interest in rogues and itinerant people, published a tract on the subject in 1566. In this *Caveat for Common Cursitors* he describes in great detail the lives, ways and language of vagabonds in order that 'these peevish, perverse, and pestilent people begin to fret, fume, swear, and stare at this my book, their life being laid open and apparently painted out'. He thoroughly approved of the measures taken against Gypsies and was of the opinion that they were not only beneficial but also successful against:

> the wretched, wily, wandering vagabonds calling and naming themselves Egyptians, deeply dissembling and long hiding and covering their deep, deceitful practices, feeding the rude common people, wholly addicted and given to novelties, toys, and new inventions; delighting them with the strangeness of the attire of their heads and practising palmistry to such as would know their fortunes; and, to be short, all thieves and whores, as I may well write. As some have had true experience, a number can well witness, and a great sort hath well felt it. And now, thanks be to God, through wholesome laws, and the due execution thereof, all be dispersed, banished, and the memory of them clean extinguished; that when they be once named hereafter our children will marvel what kind of people they were.

For the rest of the century further laws were enacted against 'rogues, vagabonds and sturdy beggars' and in 1609 a house of correction was ordered to be built in every county to accommodate those found guilty of vagrancy. During the 1760s antagonism between Gypsies and the authorities increased and in March 1761 some of a 'large gang' of Gypsies were convicted of felony and sent to Maidstone Gaol together with another one for burglary. In October 1762 Maidstone Quarter Sessions ordered peace officers to be particularly vigilant as 'several dangerous gangs of vagrants pretending to be Gypsies and tell fortunes' were infesting various parts of the county and committing enormities'. 1500 copies of the order were printed and put up in every parish in the West Kent division.

In 1766 the Justices at Wingham expressed worries that:

> many idle and disorderly persons, commonly called Gypsies, have lately been guilty of stealing horses, and other felonies in or near the county of Kent, several of whom have been apprehended and committed to Gaol, and many others are now lurking about, and secreting themselves in the eastern parts of the said county.

The justices ordered two advertisements to be printed in the Canterbury newspaper, the *Kentish Post* directing 'all constables, borsholders, and other peace officers, within the said Division to

Galician Gypsies being moved from Wandsworth common, 1911

make diligent search for, and to take and apprehend all such persons called Gypsies and carry them before one of his Majesty's Justices of the Peace to be dealt with according to the Law.'

A variety of legislation continued to enter the statute books until 1783 when the 1530 Act was repealed as being excessively severe. The general legislation against vagrants remained in force until the early nineteenth century when most of it was tidied into one act in 1824. Over the years, individuals could suffer all manner of punishments, including whippings, beatings, ear-boring, incarceration or being pressed into the Navy. However, it seems that Gypsy Travellers tended to escape these punishments: they were financially self-supporting and also travelled in large groups, making it difficult for representatives of authority to apprehend them.

Although over the centuries the level of persecution gradually fell, this was not true everywhere. The penalties for vagrancy were harsh in Britain, but latterly they were not as punitive as those applied in many countries in mainland Europe. The last execution in the UK simply for being a Gypsy took place in Suffolk in the 1650s, but in many other countries the sanction continued. In 1725 Frederick William I of Prussia decreed that all Gypsies were to be hanged and in 1726 a similar

Milos Tchoron,
London, 1911

law was passed in Spain. In Berne in 1727 all Gypsies were to have an ear cut when they were caught and be put to death if caught again, whilst in Aachen a similar ordinance passed in 1728 condemned all Gypsies to death. Floggings, deportations and the forcible removal of children remained across Europe as common punishments simply for being Gypsy. In Holland and Denmark 'Gypsy Hunts' were still officially sanctioned in the eighteenth century and as late as the 1860s Gypsies were still being legally bought and sold in the slave markets of Romania. The owners of these slaves also had the right to summarily execute any of his possessions without recourse to the law.

The gradual easing of the more punitive legislation in these countries in the latter part of the nineteenth century was one factor that allowed new migrations of Gypsies across Europe. Many travelled to France, Germany and the Netherlands and in 1886 a large group of coppersmiths arrived in Liverpool, some of whom had come from as far afield as Greece, Romania, Serbia, Bulgaria and Turkey. Over the next few decades there were reports of bands of Hungarian, German and Romanian Gypsies turning up in various parts of the country. Most of these were large groups with a high profile but we will never know how many individuals or families quietly arrived on our shores to escape persecution on the mainland. Many Scandinavian and central European countries still maintained punitive legislation against Roma until well into the twentieth century and, until the instigation of the 1905 Aliens Act, immigration into Britain comparatively easy for those seeking a better life. Although life here for Travellers was hard and harassment commonplace, it was certainly better than in many other European states. Kent has always been one of the major gateways to the British Isles and for those who cross the Channel from mainland Europe, the county provides their first experience of England. This may be another factor contributing to Kent's high Traveller population: any Roma that made the crossing from mainland Europe would immediately find themselves in an area with an existing Gypsy community and a good supply of work suited to the Travelling lifestyle.

CHAPTER TWO

Horse-drawn Days

———

For most of the nineteenth century Gypsies were still travelling in light carts or on foot. Although the image of the
wagon as a wooden house on wheels still persists as an icon of
Gypsy culture, historically it was only in use for about a hundred years. Travelling showmen were the first to recognise the
value of specialist horse-drawn vans which could be built to
serve a number of purposes. At the beginning of the nineteenth
century several showmen were using specially constructed
horse-drawn vehicles to transport their animals and very soon
some began experimenting with custom-built living wagons. These
caravans were probably made and supplied by the manufacturers

Family with brush wagon and bender tent stopping at West Wickham near Abbey Wood

Bender tent, St Mary Cray, 1870

of specialist fairground equipment and built to the requirements and design of each individual customer. But by the
1860s a more universal style had evolved that we would now
recognise as a typical horse-drawn caravan. However, it wasn't
until the latter part of the century that Gypsies began using
them in any numbers, preferring instead to stick to their traditional ways, travelling with carts and sleeping in tents. These
'bender' tents were of an ancient form, constructed from thin,
supple hazel rods pushed into the ground, bent over and covered with sailcloth, canvas or other heavy material. They could
be made as a simple dome, perhaps just large enough to sleep
in for a night, or as much more complex structures with a central living area with a fireplace and several 'rooms' adjoining.
Sometimes the central communal space was similar in construction to a native American tepee – conical, with an opening
at the top to allow smoke from the fire to escape. When Gypsy
Travellers began using living wagons in the latter part of the
nineteenth century, the tents were not entirely abandoned but
remained in use to provide additional sleeping space for large
families. The other space that could be utilised was beneath the
wagon: a heavy canvas tilt could be attached around its base to
provide a skirt, effectively creating another bedroom.

> We were born in a tent alongside the road, a bender. What they used to
> do was to cut hazel suckers out of a wood: they'd stick them in the

Family outside their bender on Mitcham common, 1881

ground and they'd bend them over and tie them together. Then they'd
chuck a sailcloth over the top of them and they'd get a hop poke or
something similar and fill it up with straw out of the haystack and that
would be the mattress to lay on and make the bed on it for the kiddies.
You had to know what you were doing of in those days because otherwise you'd starve. You would find yourself in the workhouse. All the
skills that they knowed was passed down from their fathers, and his
fathers passed it all down to him.

Ambrose Cooper

There was ten of us in family, mother had ten and my brothers used to
lay underneath the wagon with the tilt pulled round, and the girls used
to lay up in the wagon, where they put some on the floor, some under
the bed. My father used to get up at break of daylight, light a fire, and
then my mum would get up and take all the kids out and they'd all
have whatever there was to eat at that time. And she'd wash them round
the fire, sometimes it wasn't a wash with a bowl of water, it was a drop
of cold tea poured on the corner of an old rag and wiped the children's
faces round.

Minnie Ripley

Years ago, it didn't matter where you went, you could get a job on a
farm. There was plenty of work. As soon as you left one farm, you was
on another. When you had your horse-drawn caravans, you never had no
worries whatsoever, you never had no insurance to pay for motors, no

Ornate interior of a traditional Gypsy wagon or 'vardo'. Edward and Phamie Cooper with their son Charlie on Belvedere Marshes, 1938

tax. All we had to worry was to save to put a set of horseshoes on. We know we roughed it but that time of day we had no worries whatsoever.

Mark Hilden

We lived in one small wagon, whatever one we had at the time, but they were only small. We'd get up in the morning and we'd come out round the fire and we'd live round that fire all day. Live outside, didn't matter about the weather; it could be snowing, raining and we'd just be out there all day. I think we were harder for it, happier for it.

Joe Ripley

In the days of the horse-drawn wagon, life was lived under the open sky. It was an outdoor existence with the fire as a focal point. After a day's work it was where the extended family came together to eat and turn over the day's events. It was around the fire that the youngsters listened to the stories and songs of their elders. Traditionally, the written word has never played a significant part in Gypsy life: it is essentially an oral culture in which language is fluid, flexible and free from the constraints of printed permanence. When knowledge and

The Hilding family on a hop farm

wisdom are not stored in libraries or acquired through formal education, the oral tradition has its own cultural storehouses and means of transmission.

Storytelling is one method of retaining, interpreting and transmitting knowledge. This tradition involves not only the delivery of well-rehearsed stories, it depends as much on the development of contemporary parables as it does on the repetition of older narratives. Stories are related of how people extricated themselves from tight corners or outwitted the Gorjer, and tales of overcoming hardship or hunger as well as stories of life long ago, within all of which is embedded a common understanding that reinforces cultural bonds. Of course there are some traditional folk tales in which the characters and plot remain relatively unchanged, but the storyteller is an improviser, embellishing, exaggerating and modifying the tale in response to the listener. The act of delivery is as important as the content; the storyteller needs to be quick-witted and able to develop the tale, qualities which are important in the Traveller lifestyle and necessary for survival on the road.

Left to Right: Bill Reynolds, Elsie Beaney, Caroline Smith, Minnie Jones, Harry Beaney and Pickles Beaney

In the evening, the fire provides a focus and creates a environment in which people come together and turn over the day's events, whilst stories, together with music, song and dance, inform and entertain. These songs and tunes are also part of a living and continuously developing tradition, as each generation adds new material to the family repertoire while the older songs and tunes fade from memory. These traditions are participatory, the act of sharing and inclusion are as important in maintaining the culture as is the content of the repertoire.

Of a night my uncle, Henry was his name, he used to get his old fiddle out and we'd all have a song and a tap dance. I mean, when you get kids round an old camp fire, I can remember some lovely times, a few hedgehogs round a fire cooking and you couldn't wait until they'd get done so you could have a good feed off them. I mean, the Travellers never had nothing else for entertainment, it's something to be remembered.

Minnie Ripley

Minty Smith with children, 1960s

The only things people did themselves to occupy their minds was telling stories and playing all sorts of games of a daytime, nip cap and things like that. That was a piece of wood with a point on each end of it and you'd hit it with a stick and you'd knock it in the air and see how far you could knock it. Similar game to golf, that was the old Gypsy game, nip cap they'd call it. Throwing horseshoes was another one, for instance, throwing horseshoes on a peg. There was loads of different games we'd play, then there was headn'ms, two's up, have a game of penny pitch. The only time you see games of headn'm now is up the Derby Day at Epsom.

Ambrose Cooper

We used to live off the land, we used to eat stinging nettles, snails, hedgehogs, rabbits, pheasant. We used to make our own medicine and we used to make our own ointment. See, we never used to run to the doctor

37

Sarah Anne Cooper with (Left to Right) grandson Ambrose, daughters Amey and Esther and grandson Mutchi, Marden, 1955

at that time of day, we used to get what they called the old Russian Tallow and the old ones used to run that down. They used to put mustard and camphorated oil in it, they used to stir that up and let that get chilled. Then they used to fill them little shrimp bottles up for the winter. We used to make our own medicine. I remember my mum, she used to go to the market, she used to get all the bad lemons, give them a good boil, then she used to put a spoonful of Friars Balsam and a spoonful of brimstone that they used to dry the hops with. Used to get glycerine and lemon to put in with it, then used to stir that up, strain it off and put it in bottles. That's what they used to do.

Mark Hilden

Between the wars the travelling life remained much as it had for generations. It was an outdoor life and, for most Travellers, a hand-to-mouth existence. Possessions tended to be few with families just owning those things essential to life and work. It

Stopping on a Kentish farm during hop picking

was also a life led almost entirely separately from the rest of the population and its institutions – except for the unavoidable interaction that had to take place in order to earn money. Even then the relationship was at arm's length and maintained at a minimal, functional level. The only contact that most people would knowingly have with a Gypsy would be when someone tapped on their door for water or to sell a service or product. Apart from these few unavoidable financial interactions, the loose-knit Traveller community was entirely self-contained in terms of culture, language and social organisation. Disputes and injustices would be settled internally without recourse to non-Gypsy legal practice or police forces. Marriage was conducted according to traditional custom, and religious beliefs held without church attendance. The world of the Gypsy is unknown and mostly invisible to outsiders, so their understanding of it inevitably depends on a mixture of hearsay and inherited wisdom with all its exaggerations, superstition and supposition. The Gypsy lives amongst the Gorjer and understands their ways but the same is not true in reverse.

The only time that most sedentary people would deliberately

'Gypsy Lee', the niece of Urania Boswell continuing the family tradition of fortune-telling at a gala day in Danson Park, Bexley

have any kind of interaction with a Gypsy would be when having a fortune told at a fairground. Then an air of mystery was an asset to the Gypsy and the troublesome relationship between the two was reversed. For once it was the Gypsy who was perceived to have the upper hand as a guardian of ancient wisdom; it was the Gypsy knowledge and intuition that was a sought after commodity. The romantic story-book version of the traditional Romany could be fully exploited to establish and maintain this inversion; indeed some played the part to the full and perma-nently recast themselves in the exotic role that had been created for them. Those who followed this path and reinvented their image to conform to the stereo-type could then become 'Real Gypsies' in the eyes of the Gorjer.

The Boswells of Farnborough were well-known in the locality. They led a high-profile life, they were wealthy and their self-ascription as the Gypsy King and Queen of Kent gave the impression that they were at the top of a Gypsy hierarchy. Urania Boswell was a proud and flamboyant figure, regularly to be seen passing along Orpington High Street sitting atop her pony-drawn trap with the black ostrich feathers on her hat blowing in the wind. She worked as a fortune-teller and, in spite of owning property, still lived in the traditional wagon. Gypsies like the Boswells deliberately played on the romantic stereotype of the Romany and it served them well. They were well known and respected throughout the area, playing the role of flamboyant and mysterious strangers.

When Urania Boswell died in April 1933 her funeral was opulent in the best Romany tradition. A hearse drawn by six black horses headed the cortège. Hundreds of people including

Gorjers as well as Gypsies travelled considerable distances to
pay their respects or merely to
stand at the roadside to witness
the spectacle. The local paper
gave a lot of coverage to the event
as it did a year later when
Urania's son Levi died.

Levi had been living in Bromley and succumbed to bronchial
pneumonia at the age of fifty-
two. His funeral was also a grand
affair, attracting large crowds as
his mother's had done. On 9 February 1934 the *Orpington & Kentish
Times* described the funeral:

Urania Boswell of Farn-
borough, reading a
palm, 1920s

> The funeral cortège started from Wal-
> ters Yard, Bromley, and large numbers
> of sightseers gathered there in the
> afternoon to watch the procession
> leave. The large hearse, topped with
> nodding black plumes was drawn by
> six coal-black horses, each draped
> with a purple pall and an outrider
> dressed in a velvet suit and jockey cap
> rode at the front. The coffin was
> heaped high with masses of wreaths
> and flowers, notable among them
> being a huge wreath in the shape of a
> horseshoe with a whip and a horse's head from his daughter and her
> husband. Behind the hearse followed his own pony, Nigger, led by Mr
> Leonard Lee, a cousin of Mr Boswell. Behind this again came two
> coaches drawn by a pair of black horses, draped in purple, and these were
> followed by a large number of gipsy relatives on foot.

The report continues, describing the passage of the 'sombre
cavalcade' through the town where crowds lined the streets to
pay their last respects. The acceptance of the Boswells could
give the impression that there was no antagonism between
Gypsies and the rest of the population, but the family were
very much the exception. They had become settled and had
modified their lives to fit in with sedentary ways, whilst for the
vast majority of Gypsies their lifestyle and the seasonal pattern

Crowds lining Farnborough High Street as Levi Boswell's cortège passes

Wash day

of their work had changed very little. Most families still travelled, relying on horses and living in the traditional wagon or vardo. The extended family was still the main social unit,

42

providing a good system of care and support for the very young and very old and an efficient team when working on the farms. Skills and finances were shared and life's experiences interpreted and recounted from old to young in the oral cultural tradition. But in spite of the outward appearance of romance and freedom, the Gypsy life was still synonymous with hardship. For most it was still very much a hand-to-mouth existence, supplementing earnings from farm work by selling small craft items. It was usually the women who worked from door to door selling sprigs of lucky heather, pegs and primrose baskets as they tended to be more favourably received than the men.

Jasper Smith making pegs

Used to get up in the morning and go out with my mum, used to sell all the pegs and then get the money to get the food with and then come back and help her fry it on the outside fire. I can always remember that, going getting the wood and making the fires and putting the old iron pot on and cooking all the food. We had to get out and do all the washing on the old scrubbing boards with a scrubbing brush and that. It was a really, really hard life and tough to live for the women.

Sarah Hilden Snr

Got married and got ourselves a horse and a van. I went out hawking all day long while he was at home looking after the kids and the horses. We had to do the best we could, like our dads and mums had to. When you had a young baby, you had to make a sling, fold it up, put it in it and go walking, perhaps you had no money to catch a bus. You had to go walking with your basket up your back and your baby in your arms,

43

tapping the doors to get them something to eat. So that's how it went on, no money, you had no money. You just went out and managed to rake up enough to get a bit of shopping for your kids through making things; pegs, flowers and primrose baskets, anything that come our way, that's what we done.

Louie Cooper

Not only was earning a living on the road difficult, it was made much harder by entrenched police harassment that was often quietly (if unofficially) sanctioned by superior officers turning a blind eye. It was invisible to the outsider who generally never saw past the romantic veil, but relentless for those that experienced it. In the same issue of the local newspaper that carried the sympathetic report of Levi Boswell's death in 1934 and the description of the 'sombre cavalcade' through the town where crowds lined the streets to pay their last respects, there was a short paragraph and photograph at the bottom of the front page:

CARAVAN DWELLERS MOVED ON

A small colony of caravan dwellers, who frequently visit Orpington during the year, endeavoured while trekking to encamp on the grass verge of Court Road last week. Their object was to trade with residents of Orpington, but the police were asked to interfere and move them onto another parish. There were about six caravans and other vehicles used by the colony. The police issued an order to the colony to leave Orpington "at once" and escorted them in the direction of Green Street Green to see that they would obey the order.

The newspaper report describes the people who were 'moved on' as 'caravan dwellers', a description which denied their status and made it possible to justify the action taken

The eviction in Court Road, Orpington in 1934 was a typical operation of its time. The police would gather together a gang of men from the nearest town or village to assist with the eviction. These often took place at night or late evening, regardless of whether all the family members were present at the time. A man or woman coming home from a day's work might return to find the stopping place empty. In this instance the woman is clearly distraught, sometimes the wagons would be rolled off with the children still inside. The vehicles and their contents could also be badly damaged by rough handling against them. Unlike the Boswells, they were not considered to be 'real Gyspies' and could therefore be treated in this peremptory manner. The report also gives the impression that they were simply ordered to leave, but the other photographs taken at the same time but not published tell a different story, one which would still be recognised by most Travellers (see p. 45).

My mother used to go out selling clothes pegs and that and by the time she came back the police had all shifted us. We had to go and find my mum. She'd come back to another place. It would always happen, all the time us kids would all be round the fire and the old police used to come, made us move, next place, follow us behind. Next place, pull off. 'Come on, I want you to shift again,' all hours of the night, all the children in the bed, the police used to make them move in the middle of the night. No, they didn't care.

Albert Cooper Snr

There used to be a policeman in Yalding years ago and they used to get in the back room of the Two Brewers, y'know. After they'd had a good skinful and they was more or less drunk, they'd say, 'Let's go up there and give the Gyspies a good towsing'. They used to beat them up, they'd kick your door open and there may be young ladies laying up the floor of the caravan, but the police would just barge in, they had no respect for who was in the caravan and who wasn't.

John Matthews

You see, you can't win with the law. We used to move about eight o'clock at night in the winter, they'd make you move. Well, probably when you'd got out of his beat, you was in another beat and there was a copper waiting for you there to drive you onto another beat. That's how it was that time of day, they'd kick the fire over, throw the grub off from the fire.

Mark Hilden

You may be cooking your meal in the pot, you know, hanging on a kettle crane and they'd kick it off the kettle crane, they would. That would be your meal for the day and that would be gone. You know, a lot of cases you could pick it up and wash it off because you had to and then re-cook it. This time I'm talking about was through the wartime so all food was on ration, so it was hard to find. You'd have to go and ask for a few bacon bones, pieces of bacon, pork rind, anything like that, oddments that the butcher may have left over.

John Matthews

Travellers from Erith marsh, Belvedere, 1919

Belvedere Marsh

During the winter months there was little temporary work available on farms, maybe some hedging, ditching or other labouring work, but most farmers were hard pressed to find enough for their full-time employees to do. It was customary for Travellers to find a suitable stopping place close to the means of making a living. Frequently these were on the edges

Corke's Meadow, 1955, a permanent stopping place since 1921

of towns from where goods and services could be offered to the local population. Here too they could pick up enough odd jobs amongst the urban population to supplement the summer earnings and see them through until spring. In addition to the doorstep-selling by the women, the men would seek temporary labouring work, such as tree-pruning, or call the streets with a grinding barrow, sharpening knives, scissors and shears.

In the early 1900s Belvedere, which has long since been engulfed by London's southern urban sprawl, was a small Kentish village on the Thames estuary. The adjacent marshes between there and the town of Erith had long provided a winter stopping place for Travellers coming up from rural Kent. It was convenient for access to the capital, the land was of little use for anything else and its proximity to the river and the attendant danger of flooding rendered it unsuitable for housing or industrial development. By the 1930s a permanent Traveller settlement had established itself on the marshes and Erith Borough Council began to discuss ways to clear the encampment.

Corke's Meadow, St Mary Cray (TOP)

But in spite of pressure from local residents, their plans were never carried out. Another attempt was made to close the camp in 1943 but again the council backed down, probably because it would have been faced with the difficult task of finding alternative accommodation within the borough for those who owned their plots or carried out business there.

There was another large camp at Corke's Meadow in St Mary Cray. This was owned by a local haulier and coalman, William or 'Billy' Corke who had originally purchased the land in 1921 to use as a brickyard and general storage area. Two years later he erected a toilet block, provided a standpipe, installed mains drainage and turned it into a permanent caravan site; before long it had become a semi-permanent home for dozens of families. There were also several other large, established stopping places around the fringes of south east London, at Abbey Wood, Footscray and Ruxley. Some families had arrangements with the owners of private yards further into town, to stay over winter, while others simply fared the best they could on odd corners of waste ground or commons.

Ruxley chalk pit, 1947 (TOP)

Elsewhere in Kent there were more permanent stopping places on the edges of towns and urban areas. These included places like the Darland Banks alongside Ash Tree Lane above Chatham where Travellers had stopped since the nineteenth century. The traditional round of summer work and winter stops had sustained the Travellers for generations and in spite of the usual difficulties life was predictable and followed the old pattern. The gathering clouds of war in the late 1930s heralded not only international conflict but also changes to the Travellers' way of life more profound than anyone could have foreseen.

CHAPTER THREE

Winds of Change

_____

There was twenty-five thousand of us fought in the Second World War. I was there, I had two brothers there, I had a brother dropped seven hundred miles behind the Jap line in gliders, they did the impossible to stop them getting to Port Moresby. I had a brother, he was an ambulance driver in the Middle East, a field ambulance. I was in it three year and a half and we came out of Dunkirk. And when we came home, what did they do? Stuck big notices up in the pub windows, 'No Gypsies served', and that's how we came to be in trouble, a lot of us, for smashing pubs up over it.

Mark Hilden

At the outbreak of the Second World War Britain was importing vast quantities of produce from the Commonwealth, but the new threat to the merchant fleet meant that this chain of supply was to be broken. The government very quickly realised that the nation came nowhere near to being able to feed itself and instigated a number of initiatives to address the

Moses Brazil with his children Mary, Jo & Moses, 1956

Smith family hopping in the late 1950s. Great Cheveny Farm, Marden

dilemma. Through the *Dig for Victory* campaign every scrap of fertile land came under cultivation; the land army was formed to help farmers raise their productivity, and tractors increasingly replaced horses. After the war, vowing that they would never be caught out again, the government continued with the task of improving agricultural efficiency.

Herbicides became more sophisticated, reducing the need for hand weeding, and picking machines were developed for a wide range of crops. The new generation of tractors, with their hydraulic systems, powered tools and new implements, also reduced the need for labour on the farms. Although the first hop-picking machine was seen in Kent in 1937, it wasn't until the post-war labour shortages that they really became established and by 1958 almost half of the local hop harvest was picked mechanically. Gradually, much of the farm work that Travellers had traditionally undertaken was disappearing or being done by British and foreign students. Each spring, fewer families left their winter sites to follow the traditional farm circuit, preferring to remain in the same place all year and become increasingly reliant on income derived from other forms of employment.

Wartime bombing had created an acute housing shortage and in the immediate post-war years the number of people on the large, established sites had increased considerably as more former house-dwellers joined these traditional Gypsy communities. Amongst them were de-mobbed soldiers, perhaps experiencing emotional or family difficulties and unable to fit back into a more settled existence. There were many others made homeless by bombing or otherwise displaced by the turmoil of war. They lived in whatever they could get hold of and converted vans, lorries and buses, sheds and tents appeared next to the Gypsy caravans. During the war a considerable number of East Enders had simply upped and left London when the bombing started. They were familiar with Kent and the ways of the Traveller, having lived the outdoor life alongside them for a month every autumn during hopping.

The Baker family

In the late 1940s it was estimated that about 600 people lived on Belvedere Marsh all year round, but in winter, when the Travellers returned from their season of farm work, the number rose to about 1700. By 1951 the local newspaper estimated that about 250 people were living on Corke's Meadow in St Mary Cray in at least a hundred caravans, old vehicles and sheds, although this number also fluctuated according to seasonal work patterns. The growth of these permanent stopping places and the continuation of the old Travelling ways into the post-war era was causing concern in both local and national government. Every aspect of life in modern Britain was being overhauled in the desire to bring high standards of living as well as access to education and healthcare to everyone – including those who had hitherto stood outside the system.

Belvedere Marsh

Norman Dodds was one of the new wave of Labour politicians who took their parliamentary seats for the first time in the 1945 election. His Dartford constituency included the marshes in Belvedere and he took a keen interest in the welfare of the community who lived there. It was the first time that Gypsies and Travellers had had an ally in Parliament and in 1950 he began to take up their cause with various government ministers. His tenacity led to him being granted permission in 1951 for an adjournment debate to air the problems that Travellers were having in finding stopping places. He suggested that a party of Travellers should be invited to a meeting with Hugh Dalton, the Minister of Local Government and Planning, to discuss the situation. And so it was that a deputation of Travellers including, amongst others, William Baker and his brother Daniel Coates from Corke's Meadow and a man by the name of Anderson from Belvedere Marsh met with Dalton on 9 May 1951.

When Labour lost the general election in October 1951 the MP for Bromley, Harold Macmillan, became Minister for Housing, and although he was unwilling to instigate a national survey of the 'Gypsy problem' he did commission a study to be undertaken by Kent County Council. This included making two counts of the number of Travellers in the county, documenting their ways of earning a living, investigating school attendance and examining the conditions of their permanent sites.

Corke's Meadow, St Mary Cray

In February 1952 eighteen camps across the county, housing a total of 1,123 people, were visited. This exercise was repeated in August and again during the hopping season when it was found that the number of people in the permanent camps had decreased to 671, although the total number of nomadic persons in the county had risen to 2,427. The report also stated that the number of 'true Romanies' in Kent was probably only a small percentage of the total number of Travellers or nomads. There is no mention of the criteria that they applied in order to come to this surprising conclusion, or how they decided that the total number of 'Romanies' in the winter camps was a mere 124.

Brian Vesey Fitzgerald, who had previously written a book about the Gypsies of Britain, was asked to comment on the report's findings. He praised it for drawing a distinction between 'true Romanies' and other Travellers, but criticised it for suggesting that eleven Romanies lived on Corke's Meadow, because in his opinion there were none. His comments relating to the distinctions between Romanies and other Travellers were supported by another self-ascribed 'Gypsy enthusiast', William Lamour from the London City Mission to Gypsies. He said that there were about ten people of Romany blood on Corke's Meadow but declared that, as a rule, 'the full-blooded or near full-blooded Romanichal does not get into these camps unless he is very old or has met with an accident which prevents him from travelling'. Armed with this confidence in his own ability to identify 'true Romanies', he declared that nomadism was not

Ash Tree Lane Chatham, 1950s

Ruxley pit, 1950s

in itself a definition of being a Romany and criticised the report for underestimating how many there might be in the county. He suggested that this might have been due in part to the fact that many Gypsies prefer to use the term 'Traveller' – those who did not describe themselves as 'Gypsy' would not therefore be classed as 'true Romanies'.

The Travellers would have had no reason to trust the motives of local or national government; historically they had always been at loggerheads. So when council officials

Lilly, Frankie and Leonard Friend with their cousin 'Nigger' Baker,
Corke's Meadow, late 1940s

appeared and started asking searching questions about the
numbers and whereabouts of family members, it is highly
unlikely that they would have been greeted with open arms
and full co-operation. In retrospect Norman Dodds observed
that:

Lovey James and Billy Deighton, Corke's Meadow, 1950

(*below*) Albert Pateman
in Ruxley Pit, late
1940s

to use the men with the pinstriped trousers to venture into these camps, complete with pencil and paper, was not the best way to get accurate information about the number of Gypsies on any site. Time after time we were told by real Romanies that, when asked by these strangers whether or not they were Gypsies, they said 'no' because they feared that to be registered as such could mean unnecessary trouble or victimisation for them and their families.

The Kent Branch of the National Farmers Union was also invited to contribute to the research and without exception all thirteen of their quoted comments were negative. They included quotes such as:

Men and boys from the Smith, Baker and Webb families, Corke's Meadow

Gypsies are not used by farmers in the branch area; the branch would be very much opposed to Gypsies again being brought into the area.

The difficulty was to differentiate between Gypsies (who will work) and didikies (who are lazy sneak thieves).

The neighbours of those who employ them are always glad when their employment ceases.

Most of the comments also denied or very much played down the fact that Gypsies were employed on local farms, but when the union was asked two direct questions the answers were revealing.

Q. To what extent are Gypsies of use to the farmers in Kent?
A. They are used for casual labour to an appreciable extent.
Q. Would the loss of Gypsy labour affect farmers?
A. Yes.

Collectively, the farmers of Kent recognised that they were dependent on Gypsy labour but individually they denied being so. The report also discussed problems relating to education and offered radical ideas such as exempting Gypsies from education legislation, suggesting the possibility of teaching the Romany language and providing mobile units with peripatetic teachers.

Although it was the first real attempt to make a systematic

In conversation with William Lamour, Corke's Meadow

evaluation of Travellers' lifestyles and needs, the whole exercise
was obviously flawed, as an underestimate of numbers would
certainly be in the council's short-term interest: building sites
for Gypsies was a politically difficult thing to do as the electorate were always vociferous in their opposition to them. It
was therefore politically expedient to build as few as possible.
Inevitably, the council officials were not as diligent as they
should have been in their counting as they attempted to reduce
their responsibility for Traveller accommodation. By concluding that in the county of Kent there were only 124 'real' Gypsies they could justifiably release themselves from potential
political implications. Coupled with the fact that the report's
findings were never made widely available, it becomes clear
that the whole exercise paid lip service to the problem with no
real motivation to tackle the situation head-on. The overall conclusion of the report was that no decisions could be made
locally regarding site provision or education initiatives until
there was a national policy advocating the 'preservation' of
Gypsies as a separate group or alternatively encouraging their
absorption into the general community. The buck was therefore
effectively passed back to national government.

In the immediate post-war years Erith Borough Council was

Cherry-picking lunchtime

still exploring ways to clear the camp on Belvedere Marshes. In the early part of the century the owners had originally intended to develop it for housing and had laid out roads and parcelled the land into building plots. However, there were difficulties with drainage and the attendant dangers of flooding, so the plots were rented to Gypsies and Travellers who wanted more secure winter stopping places. Over the years many families had bought their plots in the hope that this would increase their security, particularly as the council was still looking to remove them. One way in which this could be achieved was for the council to compulsorily buy them out, but in order to do so they had to have good reason. This was provided by the wartime measures aimed at addressing the food shortage which enabled compulsory purchase of land for allotments. During the war a survey was undertaken amongst local residents to ascertain the demand for permanent allotments: they received 149 applications and having thus proved a need they began serving orders on the inhabitants of the marsh. The process was slow and fraught: not only did the local population not want the Gypsies on the marsh but they didn't

(*above left*)Mick Butler
with his son Jimmy
cherry picking, Sitting-
bourne, 1930s

(*above right*) Noah and
Louisa Ackleton with
daughter Louie hop
picking

Heading south down
Polhill on the A21,
from south London to
rural Kent

want them anywhere else in the locality. The task of resettling
them was inevitably hampered by the lack of alternative nearby
sites. When some businesses in Electric Road, Erith had offered
land in 1947 it resulted in the submission of a petition of over

200 hundred signatures against the 'marsh dwellers' settling there. Over that winter it was estimated that there were still 1600 people living on the marsh, but the 1952 Kent County Council survey showed that, by their actions during the intervening five years, the local council had managed to reduce the numbers to just 285.

Eventually it was an act of God, rather than an act of law, that evicted the remaining Travellers. On 1 February 1953, the Thames broke its banks during a violent storm and the marsh was flooded. Maximum tides and a fierce gale combined to create a serious threat to the river wall and an hour before high tide (due at 3.00 am), the river burst through and water tore across the marshes. Fortunately the Erith harbour master at the Port of London Authority had foreseen the situation and through the police managed to warn the residents just in time for them to escape.

The water rose with astonishing speed. Bill Golding recalls going up into his father's wagon to get him up and dressed but by the time he emerged and jumped down from the steps found himself in four feet of water. It was a remarkable escape as the Travellers waded through the rising flood to safety. Only a few managed to get their trailers and caravans onto higher ground before fleeing to rest centres with only the possessions they could carry. Thus it was that life on the marsh came to an end.

As the austerity and deprivation of the post-war years

Wagons, trailers and sheds under water, Belvedere Marsh, February 1953

Travellers fleeing the rising flood waters, 2.00 am 1 February 1953

Pearce, Rutherford and Turner families taking shelter in Abbey Wood railway station during the floods

gradually gave way to growing affluence, amongst house-dwellers the standard of living was improving and home ownership was becoming more commonplace. Residents on the new estates were becoming increasingly houseproud and conscious of the rise in their social standing and of the appearance of their neighbourhood. There was also a real desire to clear up after the war and to create a better living environment. The old

The aftermath

Corke's Meadow, 1950s

overcrowded slums were being torn down and spacious new houses and streets were being built to replace them. The permanent camps and their Gypsy occupants that had been largely tolerated before the war were now being regarded as unacceptable in the new aspirational climate. Pressure was increasing on local councils to do something about the Travellers' stopping places, particularly as they had continued to expand with old converted buses and lorries, makeshift sheds and anything else which could provide some sort of shelter.

Life on the large stopping places was becoming more at odds with that of house-dwellers. Post-war rebuilding and improvements meant that, for the first time, many families had houses with bathrooms and indoor toilets. The cooking range and hot water copper were being superseded by gas appliances and piped hot-water systems. Post-war municipal housing aimed to provide everyone with good quality, spacious accommodation. In contrast, places like Corke's Meadow were not

Mrs Luke cooking on Corke's Meadow

changing at all; there was no prospect of improving sanitary
arrangements or rubbish-collection and caravan life was still
much the same. However, now surrounded by a new community of modern housing, it had become a valuable piece of real
estate. London County Council wanted to buy the land and
build light industry there to provide work for the occupants of
the new council estates in St Paul's Cray, largely populated by
Londoners who had been moved from slum-clearance areas in
the inner city. Although the site had been a traditional stopping
place for about thirty years and the Travellers were living there
legally and paying rent, in August 1951 the owner gave them
just seven days to quit, after which the water would be turned
off and the toilet block locked. Although many families had
been there since it opened and it had become their permanent
home, the threat was duly carried out. Having nowhere that
they could legally move to, the occupants had no choice but to
remain where they were but now without access to water or
basic sanitation.

Kentish Times, 31 August 1951

For two days after the water was cut off on Thursday last week, the gypsies were unable to make tea, but then they discovered clean springs in the old cress beds along the river Cray and began carrying water from there. Mrs L Capie gave birth to a baby in a caravan on Saturday and water was carried some distance from a prefabricated house. The baby is doing well ... Chislehurst and Sidcup Council on Tuesday served notice on the owner of the land, Mr R W Corke of Hearns Rise, St Mary Cray, to abate 'the public health nuisance' at the camp...

Later it was understood that a water supply was being provided yesterday by means of a stand pipe on the highway land at Leeson's Hill just outside the camp...

The water was eventually restored, so this crude attempt to get rid of the residents of Corke's Meadow not only failed but the numbers continued to increase. By 1957 the local paper reported that 600 people were living there. In interviews broadcast on the BBC Home Service in February, residents of the meadow described the difficulties they were having trying to maintain cleanliness and hygiene in overcrowded and impoverished conditions. One mother ('whose tumbledown shack was immaculate, she had even hung pretty curtains in a pathetic attempt to make it look like a home') told radio listeners about the 'roughs' who caused trouble to the more peaceable of the dwellers and of the other menace – the rats. The place had become a shanty town where the residents were finding it increasingly difficult to maintain the lifestyle that they wanted. A few months later, the local council served notices to quit and simultaneously offered accommodation in nearby prefabs to anyone who wanted it, but there was no offer to provide an alternative site for those who wished to remain in caravans. The prefabs were in the adjoining road, Leeson's Hill, and were becoming vacant as the previous occupants moved into newly built council houses elsewhere. Although it was a solution, it didn't meet with universal approval and local residents protested about the plan which would mean that they would still have virtually the whole community of Corke's Meadow on their doorstep. At a council meeting about 150 of them staged a protest and had to be removed from the public gallery by police. Together with some local councillors they wanted the Traveller community to be split up and scattered. Councillor G H Kirby-Smith thought it was better to abide by the adage, 'divide and rule'.

The Smiths and Eastwoods waiting on Gravesend Quay for the ferry to Essex after hopping in Kent, September 1955

I was ten when I moved out of Corke's Pit, because we moved into pre-fabs. We were there three years so I was thirteen when I left that area. Corke's was alright as a stopping place but it was a bit rough. It was mainly Travellers. We had caravans but we had a big lo-decker bus that we lived in at that time, there weren't mobiles [mobile homes] then, it was just horse-drawn caravans or caravans you could tow, small ones. So we were living in a bus for a room; there were also sheds there. There was only one tap and a block of four toilets at the top and where we stopped it must have been about a quarter of a mile away so you had to walk for water, or cart water from that block of toilets. There was no wood or anything so you had to cart wood in there. At this time there wasn't any dustcarts come round so people had to get rid of their rubbish the best they could but there was an old dump on there that a lot of people dumped their rubbish on. They came and offered the chance of going into prefabs — most people were pleased to go into them but they regretted it afterwards. But those that were left, they just pulled them out because there weren't enough prefabs for everyone. Just pulled them out and left them.

Joe Ripley

Wrotham Heath at the foot of the North Downs, apple picking time in
the late 1940s. This was a popular stopping place which allowed the
horses to have an overnight rest before tackling Wrotham Hill

Although there have always been individual Travellers who have
moved in and out of houses, this incident was the first real
attempt at larger-scale settlement. Inevitably some remained in
the prefabs, eventually transferring to permanent housing, but
for others it was a transition that was to prove too difficult to
sustain. For them the cultural, social and practical changes that
they had to undergo proved to be emotionally insurmountable
and eventually many of those who had accepted accommodation gave it up and returned to a life of harassment on the
roads, chasing after an ever-decreasing pool of temporary farm
work.

> *This time of year coming along now we used to look for work, agricul-*
> *tural work, fruit picking, hop picking, potato picking up, you can't get it*
> *now, it all finished. They're all mechanical-wise, the likes of cherries,*

Noah Ackleton and Georgie Eastwood with their new Bedford truck

plums, apples, you may get a job at that, but it's very rare because they've only got enough to keep their own locals going.

Mark Hilden

As from the Sixties onwards, they was inventing more things like hop machines and so on and various other machines to do other work. They was cutting the Gypsies out and having students in to do the work. As they cut the farm work out then we had to go, winter and summer, calling for scrap, tree-lopping, tarmacking, dung-selling, loads of logs and so on, all sorts of things in order to try and earn a bit of money. Going from the Fifties into the Sixties, there was a change: some Gypsies had wagons, some Gypsies had trailers, caravans, some had horses and some had old 'O' type lorries. We could travel, but as soon as the villagers started on you and they ganged up on you, and they'd want you out of it, we used to hook on and move because we didn't want no trouble. We used to move anywhere and we was free, we was free, and that's the way we wanted it really.

Jack Hilden

The transition from a horse-drawn existence to a lorry and trailer was traumatic but inevitable. The relationship between

Tommy Collins, Noah Collins, Noah Ackleton

Gypsy and horse is ancient and deep, but as the farms had become mechanised and the amount of available labouring work fell, so the Travellers followed suit and became motorised. In many ways, though, the trailer did bring about an improvement in the quality of life: it was more spacious and had gas lighting, heating and cooking. In bad weather the whole family could more easily share the space and keep warm and dry, and the motor vehicle brought new possibilities for employment. Any job that involved haulage or the removal of waste became viable and it was also possible to travel further afield in search of work.

If you want to go from here to, say, Essex you could hook on and you'd be there in an hour, but if you was horse-drawn you couldn't get there until a couple of days. You could get further afield with a trailer and a vehicle. You could travel from here and go to Cambridge potato picking up, Wales, Herefordshire we used to go, hop picking. Lincolnshire, Norfolk. We worked on the Queen's place at Kings Lynn, that was one of the biggest blackcurrant farms she had.

Mark Hilden

The Smith and Cooper families around the fire at hopping. The young Albert Cooper is proudly showing off the bike that his dad put together from old bits and pieces including an old pram wheel on the front

Me dad only give thirty pound for the first trailer we had and I remember it was more like a wagon because the draw bar was at one end and the back door was at the other, so it was more like a wagon than the first one we had. We pulled it with an old Bedford lorry, I think it was, and I thought it was something to be really, really proud about. Of course as we got on and I got older and I got mixing with the people who did have money, they always looked down on us and they'd say, 'What an old trailer or caravan or whatever they used to call it, what a load of rubbish'. And to me it was just, y'now, 'I'm proud of it', compared to what I used to have, you know, a tent, or a wagon, laying underneath the wheels. It's like a million-dollar thing to me.

Sarah Hilden Snr

Modern technology was beginning to make itself felt in other areas too. The fire had always provided a social arena. It was here that the participatory and inclusive traditions of music, singing and storytelling were maintained, but now new, passive forms of entertainment were creeping in.

Annie Scamp and Betsy Eastwood on Darland Banks, Ash Tree Lane,
Chatham, 1950s

I remember when I was a little girl, I was only about six or seven years
old, we used to go on a farm, hopping. It was Great Cheveney Farm,
Marden, we used to go there for years and years. I remember we used to
go shopping with our mums and we'd look through a house window in
the village and we'd see a telly, five or six kids at a time would be looking through this lady's window at the telly. I suppose she got fed up
with us and just pulled the curtains, but we still went on that we
wanted a telly. The men went and got some big old electric tellies and
they was made of, like a stained mahogany stuff – these big old tellies
with a dear little old screen. We had one with no picture on, but the
sound, and one with no sound but a picture and we had one sitting on
the other one. The farmer said 'you can put the tellies in the barn',
because that was the only way of getting electric. Because we used to live
right over in the field and there wasn't no electric. So, anyway, they
rigged these two tellies up and we had one for the picture and one for the
sound, but you had to have them tuned into the same station. All us kids
used to go running over to Mr Day's barn to the telly and we used to sit
all amongst the straw and get all comfortable and watch the telly, but
we used to watch anything, what was ever on it we was interested in, oh
dear, years and years ago.

Minnie Ripley

The Rye family living in a farm shed and vardo, Crockenhill, 1947

In the desire to clear up after the war and to build a brave new world, not only were the houses that had been destroyed by bombing during the war being replaced but old sub-standard housing and slums were also being cleared. Legislation was enacted to ensure that all new houses should have rooms of a certain size, ceilings of a minimum height, indoor toilets, hot-water systems and damp-proof courses – in future an entire set of minimum standards would have to be observed. In addition, the Town and Country Planning Act of 1947 ensured that development was to be properly controlled not just to prevent urban sprawl and ribbon development, but also to curtail the growing pre-war shanty towns that had grown up in places like Biggin Hill, Knatts Valley and Happy Valley near Meopham. Before the

The Ball family's trailers and wagon in Ruxley pit

war speculators had carved these areas into 'leisure plots' for weekend escapees from London who had put caravans on them, or else built shacks, wooden bungalows or ingeniously converted buses or railway carriages. During the post-war housing shortage, many of these places provided permanent homes for those who had been bombed out or who had simply sought to escape the Blitz. These areas were never intended to provide permanent accommodation and they were exactly the kind of thing the planning authorities wanted to prevent in the future: most of the buildings were flimsy wooden structures, the roads were unmade, mains drainage non-existent and the buildings sprawled randomly into the countryside.

Late 1960s, stopping at Pratts Bottom on the A21 near Orpington

Planning and building legislation which was enacted with the best intentions of ensuring that the population was well housed in a good environment also equipped local authorities with ammunition to use against Travellers and anyone else who chose not to live under a tiled roof supported by bricks and mortar. The traditional camps that Travellers had moved between could now be prevented or cleared under the new legislation and permanently stationed caravans classed as substandard accommodation. Earlier legislation was also being increasingly enforced, so that camps with very basic or no sanitation and no permanent water supply could be construed as contravening the Public Health Act of 1936. The net was closing in on the Travelling culture, traditional ways of earning a living were disappearing and finding somewhere to stop was becoming increasingly difficult.

> I remember the time we used to stop on farms for round about a couple of months and he wanted us out of it because the council got onto him and we used to pull onto the side of the road, round Ashford area. Sometimes we used to go over the county into Maidstone and go to and fro, to and fro all the time. Back in the Sixties the Gypsies used to pull off anywhere where there was enough room beside the road, or a lay-by or a bit of waste council ground alongside the roads. It was very, very hard. My mother and father had a family, they used to go out and do calling

Cockles, Faithy, Wally and Eddie Butler, Ash Tree Lane, late 1940s

The Ripley family beside the A2 at Cobham

— my mother did as well, she used to go out with a basket of flowers on her arm. Things were very, very hard, didn't know what it was to have a decent pair of shoes and a decent pair of trousers, things were poor. In those days it was up to the council to summons you, go to court and then make us move on.

Jack Hilden

You could never go back to live the way we used to because you'd end up in prison, that's what would happen to you in the finish of it. You'd just do so many things against the law today that we used to be able to do, you'd end up going in prison. All the old stopping places are done away with now, I mean the old traditional stopping places like the Springhead Arches, places like that, Mereworth Springs. What the council done, corners like that that we used to stop, as they were getting the Travellers off, they were putting banks along the front of them, or trenches, so the Travellers could never pull back on again. I mean, the Mereworth Springs, Seven Mile Lane, there's hundreds of old Travellers stopped there for water, got water out of that spring. Look at old Corke's Pit, the way that that disappeared. I was born in Corke's Pit in an old wagon. One of my aunts born me, there wasn't no nurses come there, no doctors. Travellers lived there for years, didn't they? All that was done away with, they built bungalows there, the old prefabs were there. That's where the Travellers made a mistake: from Corke's Pit, they moved into the prefabs, that was the first of Travellers settling down. When they got into them, they didn't like them. We lived in a prefab for about three years and we bought a wagon and moved back out again.

Joe & Minnie Ripley

78

Nowhere to go

T ravellers have always stopped on common land. It was not an unusual sight to see a family unit of two or three horse-drawn wagons stopping off for a night or two on the journey between farms, and they were usually tolerated because the locals knew that they would soon be on their way. Hothfield Common near Ashford was one such place. It was a large area of wooded heathland of the sort that Gypsies had always stopped on to break their journeys or for longer periods over the winter. However, because other stopping places and the number of welcoming farms were diminishing, by the winter of 1958 the common had become a permanent home for a number of families occupying about twenty caravans, whereas eighteen months before there had been only one. Not only did it appear that they were there to stay but the numbers were

Yalding Lees, late 1940s. This common was a popular stopping place for Travellers who worked the county's farms

increasing and the romantic appearance of the old-time Gypsy was changing, now that the horses and vardos were joined by lorries, trailers and vans. All were parked on the common with no prospect of finding a new place to move to that winter. Earlier legal attempts to move them had proved ineffective so West Ashford Council negotiated with the owner of the common to purchase it, with the express purpose of evicting the Travellers. In January 1959 Major A T Palmer, the chairman of the council housing committee, confirmed to the *Kentish Express* that as soon as the council had possession of the land the Travellers would be given fourteen days to leave, and any that refused to do so would be towed onto the road to be dealt with by the police. The council were reported as being concerned about possible health risks posed by the site, believing that the traditional ways of sanitation were no longer appropriate in a modern age.

Finally, in the middle of February, representatives of West Ashford Council served notice on the one hundred 'caravan dwellers' living on the common, to quit within fourteen days. At the same time, news broke that the council was considering creating a permanent site in a disused quarry at Ninn Lane in nearby Great Chart. A member of Ashford West Rural District Council (RDC), Councillor Wing Commander Lawrence had hinted at the idea the previous week when he had said: 'everyone has got to realise that we have got to find a site for these people. We have had Gypsies in this country since time immemorial. The majority have disappeared and those we have now in caravans are not true Gypsies'. He went on: 'This problem will go on and on unless we make a decision now. I do feel that wherever we put the site we will get great opposition. None of us likes having Gypsies camping on our doorsteps. The people on Hothfield common are not true 'Romanies' but 'interlopers'; they carry on businesses and should be made to have proper business premises'. His proposal for a council-owned and controlled site in Ninn Lane was accepted by the committee but sparked off a lengthy and bitter battle with Great Chart Parish Council who passed a motion of 'no confidence' in West Ashford RDC at a meeting of one hundred parishioners in the village hall. The village was up in arms at the prospect of Gypsies in their parish, not least because judging for the annual 'best kept village' competition was imminent. One local farmer predicted that they 'will make it frightfully difficult for the West Ashford RDC to establish a car avan site at Ninn Lane, and will "raise a disturbance", by trying to move the caravanners on themselves.'

In early March the eviction from Hothfield common took place and those who could not, and some who would not, move were towed onto the road by council workmen. The event was reported in the *Kentish Express*:

> Police stood by at Tuesday's eviction, but the remaining cara-
> vanners, grumbling quietly, made no real attempt to stop the
> move. Huddled up in shawls and raincoats against the rain,
> they stood by their vans, or by their piles of belongings,
> saying they had nowhere else to go. Children crowded at the
> windows to watch. A bedraggled hen sheltered under a rusty
> pram. Where a few weeks ago the common had been strewn
> with lines of washing, and children and puppies played
> together round the cooking fires, the lines of painted vans on
> the roadway, leaving heavy tracks in the mud, made a desolate
> sight.

They were moved about two miles away to a temporary site on an old rubbish tip at Chilmington. One of the Travellers, Mrs A Hilden, commented that, 'I would never have come here if I had known what it was like. I would have pulled on to the road alongside the heath.' Her husband had been ill since moving there and his doctor had written a letter to the council asking for more suitable accommodation. He added that the tip was beginning to smell, that food could not be kept there because of the flies and they were also being kept awake at night by the sound of rats. Bill Matthews was also on the site: 'It's not healthy for the children and in the summer when the flies come it will be terrible. It is not fit for the kiddies. You have to wash them three or four times a day to keep them clean.'

The fact that the new site was clearly a polluted and unpleasant place was seized on and exploited by Great Chart Parish Council. On Monday 28 May they sent five tractors there offering to move the Travellers back to Hothfield common. The offer was accepted, but within five hours West Ashford RDC handed each family notice to quit and they were immediately towed back to the Chilmington tip by Ashford Council employ-ees. A member of Great Chart parish declared that 'they were being kind to the Gypsies to move them away from a terrible place like that.' This opinion was reinforced by the chairman who said that the 'dwellers' had been moved from the tip on humanitarian grounds as it was infested with rats and flies and was considered by the council to be unfit for human habita-tion. This very public argument between the councils, which culminated in families being pushed around like pawns, finally brought some sympathy from the local paper. This episode of appalling harassment was highlighted on the front page of that week's edition in large headlines:

RAT INFESTED REFUSE DUMP IS CARAVANNERS' HOME

The ensuing article reported the day's events, concluding: 'Meanwhile, back at the refuse tip, as about fifteen children of the families crawled among empty tins and dogs scratched enthusiastically among the refuse, the caravanners were discussing their day trip to Hothfield.'

The editorial castigated both councils for their behaviour:

IN THE NAME OF HUMANITY

The desperate plight of the unhappy caravan dwellers who are being pushed from pillar to post, ending up (very temporarily we hope) on a rat-ridden refuse tip at Great Chart is one which the public should not countenance for a moment. We realise that there are good reasons for keeping caravannners off the picturesque common, and we applaud Great Chart's action in insisting that there should be none on the Chilmington refuse tip. This is the point at which we join issue. West Ashford Rural Council and Great Chart Parish Council are at loggerheads over the matter when quite obviously they have to come together in an emergency meeting to see what can be done to settle the problem on humanitarian grounds, coupled with private and public interests. It is true that the Rural District Council hopes to have a permanent site with proper amenities at Ninn Lane, Great Chart, but this may not be ready until next year. To put these wretchedly sited human beings on the list does not seem to solve the problem. We do not hesitate to say that a refuse dump is no fit place for any family, particularly when so many children are involved. With this we are sure the public will agree. A rubbish tip for human habitation in 1959? What on earth are we thinking about! We ask our readers to study the photographs on our front page and act. Tell both the councils what you think about it. The situation itself is bad enough; the argument between the two councils is deplorable. The families should never have been put on the site at all.

Over subsequent weeks the argument raged between the councils and in the columns of the local newspaper. West Ashford RDC had the site investigated by Dr J Marshal MOH who had visited Chilmington with senior public-health inspectors. They

A temporary stop over

came to the conclusion that the site was safe to live on and that conditions were no worse than on any other caravan site any-where in the country, the mess being entirely of the residents' own making. A doctor engaged by Great Chart Council inevitably had a different opinion. He observed that:

> There is no sanitation at all; the water supply is from a tap some distance away and the water is stored for each caravan in a doubtfully clean old milk churn. There is stagnant water which in warmer weather will allow the breeding of mosqui-toes. The place is congested with rubbish and rats are preva-lent. In my opinion the site is absolutely unsuitable, and disease, typhoid, typhus etc will probably arise if occupation is continued in hotter weather. The smell from the burning dump some 50 yards away is horrible, particularly when the wind is east. I would utterly condemn this site as dangerous and impossible for these people and also for the neighbours.

As always, it was not a matter of what was best for the Trav-ellers, but a matter of invisibility. They could be clearly seen on the common which was an amenity and beauty spot where local people walked their dogs and played with their children. It was recreational land and not somewhere for people to live, but in spite of the obvious dangers to health, an old household refuse tip was considered to be suitable for the Travellers. How-ever, even this inhospitable place was not destined to provide refuge for long: a week later West Ashford RDC served eviction notices on those very families that they themselves had put there six weeks earlier.

After protracted wrangling, in May 1960 the Minister of

Norman Dodds MP having his leg pulled in Dartford Woods by Joe Dennard

Housing and Local Government finally approved the land at Ninn Lane, Great Chart for residential use by Travellers. In the following months the council prepared the site. It was laid out with sand-filled bays for twelve caravans, concrete paths and clinker access roads, a permanent water supply, a toilet block and lighting supplied by hurricane lamps on wooden poles. By August, after being away for the summer work, a number of families returned to live on the edge of Chilmington rubbish tip. In spite of the vociferous and aggressive reaction of many villagers, other local residents saw no reason to object to the Travellers and were brave enough to express their opinions. The village shop and post office owner was quoted in the *Kentish Express* as saying, 'they are lovely people. They are always well mannered when they come in here. Of course I would serve them. They are all God's children'. However, the licensee of the Black Dog said that he would not serve them because if they drank regularly at his house it would have a bad effect on his custom and that he was thinking about putting a 'No Gypsies Served' notice in his window. Mr Frank Barton, a local grocer and chairman of the Great Chart Parish Council agreed. He said, 'from a personal point of view, I would rather not serve them.'

The parish council were unhappy about the presence of the Travellers and suggested that West Ashford RDC should follow the example of East Ashford RDC, who had bought up land that Travellers were living on in Chilham and fenced it off to prevent their return. Although West Ashford said that they would do nothing about Chilmington until the new site was ready, one Traveller who was stopping there, Ebeneezer Emmet, claimed that he had already been given twenty-four hours to leave. 'Where will we go?' he asked a local newspaper reporter after he had been there about a week. 'I'm sick of being pushed about like this,' he said, adding that he would be willing to move if they had somewhere to go, 'but we're always being pushed out on the road.'

Discussions at Ashford West council meetings continued regarding the management and regulation of the new site. Caravans were to be of recognised design, there would be no storage of materials or parking of trade vehicles, and no trade or business could be carried on from the site other than crafts which could be done in caravans. There was also discussion as to whether dogs should be allowed to be kept on the new site. One councillor felt they should not be because he thought they might be used for poaching. Another said that farmers of adjoining land were concerned about sheep being worried, but in the end no such restrictions were imposed and in November the first residents, the Hildens, the Lees and the Wilsons, pulled on together.

For taking this innovative step and being the first council in the country to make any such provision for Travellers, West Ashford RDC was praised in Parliament by Norman Dodds, MP for Erith and Crayford for 'its courageous and humanitarian decision which is in marked contrast with the shameful treatment of Gypsies in other parts of the country.' In reply, Sir Keith Joseph, Parliamentary Secretary for the Minister of Housing, said that the Minister welcomed the efforts of West Ashford RDC. He was then asked by Sir Godfrey Nicholson if the minister appreciated that it was widely felt that a picturesque and harmless community was in danger of being crushed by a 'rather soulless bureaucracy' and would he pay a little more

Making primrose baskets in Dartford Woods in 1959, Betsy Smith
looking on

attention to its interests in the future? He was assured by Sir Keith Joseph that the example set by West Ashford was one that might be followed.

For all its humanitarian attitude towards provision for Travellers, the council's actions were not without an additional agenda. Although the site was permanent it was not built with the intention of providing a permanent home for Travellers. The *Kentish Express* reported discussions that took place within the council regarding the formulation of a code of conduct for the site: 'Other rules, in the attempt to groom the Gypsies for eventual council-house tenancy, include the duty of keeping the ablution block clean. The twelve families will undertake this duty on a weekly rota basis.' They obviously felt that Gypsies had an intrinsically dirty lifestyle incompatible with house-dwelling and that housecraft and cleaning should be learnt by practising on the toilet block. However, more insidious than this insult was the council's aim of eventually getting the Travellers into houses and the idea that the site was a staging post where they could be groomed for their future tenancies. During August, as the council were considering who should be offered pitches, Councillor Major O W Cotton, chairman of the committee set up to select families for the site, made a suggestion which was accepted: a document should be signed by prospective tenants to the effect that they would be prepared to move into a council house later on. 'We don't want people setting up in business out there for the rest of their natural,' he declared. This message was reinforced in October when the chairman of West Ashford RDC told the *Kentish Express* that 'The all important thing is for the twelve families who will use the camp to settle down to a regular life. We hope they will get steady jobs and prepare themselves for life in a house.'

Although site provision catered for the Travellers' immediate practical needs by providing somewhere to stay, the council's declared long-term aim was to stop them from continuing their traditional nomadic lifestyle. There was no recognition of or respect for this way of life or the culture that it supported. They could see nothing of value in it; to them it was dirty, insecure and obviously inferior to living in a house and having a permanent job. The rules for the site were framed to ensure that its occupants became employees; they were not to be allowed vans or lorries or to store material that they might require for carrying out odd jobs or gardening work. Travellers had no tradition of permanent waged employment because a

In 1961 Norman Dodds and the local headmaster, Alan Poole, took a group of children from Dartford Woods to the House of Commons. Left to Right: Frank Jones, Buddy Baker, Genty Dennard, Olive Chambers, Charlotte Brown and Mary Smith

nomadic life precluded it. Most had always been self-employed on a casual basis and knew no other way. Those who made the rules did not recognise that there was any cultural difference between Gypsies and themselves and apparently felt that once the Travellers had experienced some of the benefits of permanence they would soon be persuaded to conform to sedentary ways. This stated intention for the country's very first site set the precedent for all subsequent legislation and policy regarding site provision – that there should be a process of making stopping impossible anywhere except on official sites, which should then act as a channel into housing. For many it seemed to be just another Gorjer ploy to eventually destroy the Gypsy life and they became even more adamant that they would never 'end up' on a permanent council site.

In the same year the Government introduced the Caravan

Sites and Control of Development Act 1960. So many people had taken to caravan dwelling since the post-war housing shortage that the authorities felt this form of accommodation should now be regulated. The Act was framed to regulate the activities of some unscrupulous site owners who were cashing in on the situation by providing sub-standard accommodation in return for high rents. In future they would be required to apply for a license which would only be granted if certain conditions, including the layout of the site, screening, sanitary arrangements and so on were met. The Act did allow temporary sites to be set up for agricultural and forestry workers, provided that they were only in use while the occupants were actually working. Farmers who employed Travellers for seasonal work were usually, even if begrudgingly, sympathetic to allowing them to remain for a while after picking was finished because they knew that they would shortly be moving on to the next job. Similarly, Travellers who might have arrived on a farm a week or two before they were needed didn't pose much of a problem; they were self-sufficient and ready to work as soon as the crop ripened.

Perhaps in response to the kind of situation that had evolved at Hothfield, the 1960 Act also gave rural district councils the power to prohibit caravans on the commons which had hitherto provided essential temporary stopping places between jobs or on the longer journeys back to winter accommodation. Coupled with the new rules governing temporary sites, this made life increasingly difficult for those Travellers who undertook casual agricultural work. As soon as a picking job finished the law required caravans to be moved off the farm immediately, even if the next job wasn't ready to begin for another couple of weeks, and in addition a temporary stop on a nearby common was now also illegal.

Although it was claimed that the act was intended to address concerns around 'caravan living by ordinary people, rather than the special problem of Gypsies and vagrants', it inevitably created serious difficulties for all Travellers and became yet another weapon that could be used against anyone who lived in a caravan, including the 'real Gypsies'.

Elsewhere in the county, in Darenth Woods adjacent to the A2 at Cobham, another permanent camp had been evolving and by 1960 about a hundred families were living there. Disquiet was growing amongst local residents about the presence of Gypsies in their area and Darenth Parish Council and Dartford

Site meeting at Dartford Woods with members of the parish council, Sidney Irving MP, landowners and Chief Inspector Keaven

Rural District Council were both keen to find ways of removing them. However, the wood was owned by the Church Commissioners, who presumably felt unable to evict the Travellers, so in September 1960 they made arrangements to sell the land to Darenth Parish Council. In spite of the fact that it was not in his own constituency, Norman Dodds soon took an interest in the developing situation and in November he successfully pressed the education authorities to make provision for over fifty children who were living there. But he was also suspicious about the council's motives for purchasing the wood. In an interview for the *Gravesend and Dartford Reporter* on 2 December, Dodds called on the Church Commissioners not to sell to Darenth Parish Council because he believed that once the sale was completed the Travellers would be given just seven days to leave. In the next issue of the paper, Ernest Collier, the chairman of the council, wrote a letter, displaying his resolve:

Sir,

In all the recent publicity on television and in the Press on Darenth's gipsy problems, little has been made of the large

Minty Smith in discussion with an official from Dartford Council, 1960

numbers of innocent people mostly concerned – the residents and ratepayers of the parish. Many of these have suffered – some more than once – in several ways. Lawns and gardens have been damaged by straying horses, during darkness and daylight; children have been unable to play on the greens and open spaces because of the many tethered horses. The local constable had three 'strays' tethered in his garden one night for lack of facilities for pounding them. There have been thefts of clothes and lines from gardens; peremptory demands to housewives for water or old clothes; the offer of pegs or plants for sale, when refused, has been met by a torrent of abuse and obscene language. There have been allegations of young girls molested and the beating up of men by gangs of men. The rural council's yard near the site has had to be closed on two occasions because the workmen could not work without police protection. Finally there is the spoliation

Norman Dodds looks across the earth bank thrown up around the
woods in advance of the eventual eviction

and devastation of a once beautiful wood, with the accompa-
nying filth and squalor that must be seen to be believed.

For several more weeks public argument raged in the letter
pages of the local newspaper. Dodds accused the parish and district councils of neglecting their duty to find a constructive
solution, with Collier replying on behalf of the residents of
Darenth, 'who conform to the normal standards of a civilised
community and who have to pay dearly for doing so, not only
by high rents, rates and taxes, but also by the anti-social behaviour of some of the dwellers of Darenth Woods.'

By this time the church commissioners were feeling very
uncomfortable and asked that no force or precipitous action
should be taken against the Gypsies. They also donated
£800.00, the full price that they received from the sale of the
wood, towards the cost of resettling the inhabitants. In order to
further make his point, after Christmas Norman Dodds moved
his own motor caravan into the woods and took up residence
in support of the Travellers. Then, in midwinter, on 20 January
1962, the eviction took place. Protected by the police, the
council's army of tractors moved into the woods and towed all
the caravans out onto the verge of the busy A2, badly damaging
some.

Packing up in preparation to leave the woods on the morning of 20 January 1962

We'd been in the woods about five years, about a hundred families at different times, but some used to go away fruit picking, hop picking and then come back. The church sold it to the council, I think just to move the Travellers out. Most of the local people got to know Travellers there, the pubs were a bit funny at times but they never bothered us too much because it was really out of the way there. The nearest house must have been half a mile and now they've put a motorway through, but we weren't getting a lot of trouble there. The nearest people to us were Travellers, Tommy Arber's yard, they were Travelling people, related to my wife, and no one there bothered us. We used to go down there and get water from the yard so they weren't bothered about us being there. Whatever way you came out, it was onto a main road so there were no houses there.

They just turned up in the morning [of the eviction]. There were tractors and motors to pull people out but most of them, they pulled out themselves because they knew they had to move anyway and we pulled onto the A2. They were pulling some trailers out and the jacks weren't up and all things like that. Some of the china wasn't put down and a lot of stuff got broke. In fact my mum and dad had a trailer that was broken, and a lot of china stuff, they just pulled it out as it was. They

The eviction from Dartford Woods. Those who owned caravans or
wagons without the means to move them were pulled out by council
tractors

*never gave people time to do what they wanted to do. You see, the thing is
with Travellers, they didn't think it was going to come to it that day. The
police never interfered because there was no trouble there, no violence or
anything, they were just there as a presence. We still had horse-drawn
caravans and they just pulled those out with the tractors. Most people
didn't like it, they had been in there for several years in Dartford Woods
and we were out of the way and there was no harm to the children or
anything.*

Joe Ripley

300 people were now living on the roadside within a few feet
of busy traffic. Although Norman Dodds' efforts had not prevented the eviction, he had achieved his other aim — that of

The national press in attendance ensured that the eviction was
well publicised

focusing the national media spotlight on the situation. It was
reported on BBC TV news and covered by the national press,
with particularly critical reports appearing in the *Guardian*, *The
Times* and the *Observer*. This coverage probably contributed to the
subsequent softening of attitudes in some quarters, although
neighbouring Stone parish council had always taken a different
and more constructive line than Darenth. Some factions within
Dartford RDC became increasingly unhappy about the actions
of the chairman of the planning committee, Leslie Reeves, who
had been instrumental in the whole affair. At a press conference
he had stated that it is 'our responsibility to put them out on
the highway. The Council is faced with difficult planning problems. Darenth Wood is green belt and has to be safeguarded
against infringements of the law.' When asked whether the

On the verge of the A2

middle of winter was an ideal time to evict women and children, he replied, 'We cannot hold ourselves responsible. They have brought it upon themselves, they are trespassers.'

The A2 was a very dangerous place at the time. There was a lorry came down with a load of board on and it came off and smashed three trailers. It broke them all down, there were holes in the sides that you could walk through. When they used to come down, they used to look at the Travellers. He must have been looking and he jumped the kerb and it forced the load off. It's a wonder that someone wasn't hurt there but it ruined the trailers. There were a lot of accidents because of the motors, especially at weekends. It would be really packed with traffic there and motors would come by looking and they'd run into the back of one another. Every weekend we could see accidents, minor accidents, not really serious ones, the traffic would always slow down and there'd be a lot of accidents. It was dangerous. Used to get people come through of a night throwing, hollering and shouting. They'd throw bricks or stones, whatever they had in the motor at the time. It was nothing to hear someone shouting abuse at one or two o'clock in the morning or throwing something at the caravans. You'd have the same problem wherever you went, wherever you went you had the same problem, that's why people went into places like Dartford Woods, because they are out of the way and there wasn't anyone there to bother them.

Joe Ripley

Norman Dodds in conversation with the Ripley family on the A2

After the evictions Dartford Council suffered vilification at the hands of some of the national press and there were stormy scenes at council meetings as some members realised that not all publicity is necessarily good. Reeves, however, was unrepentant and continued to justify his actions, even admitting at one meeting that he had at times acted without the full authority of the council. On 10 February 1962 it was reported in the local paper that he had answered a letter from the Ministry of Transport stating, 'that the Council could not accept responsibility for families who might, from time to time, be encamped on the roads or verges of roads within the Dartford rural district ... Any problem of this nature should be referred to the appropriate authority, which would appear to be the Ministry of Transport and the County Council.'

On the side of the A2

And later in the same council meeting he had declared that, 'You can't have these people in the community and good planning.'

The same edition of the *Reporter* carried a report on a Strood District Council meeting during which the housing manager Mr N Rees had commented on applications for houses from caravan dwellers:

> Following the consideration of applications received from occupiers of residential caravans, Strood RDC was recommended to agree that all future applicants should be informed that unless there were exceptional circumstances, applications would not be accepted for inclusion on the Council house waiting list unless the applicants had resided in the caravans within the rural district for five years. But at Friday's council meeting Mr J A Luck asked how this decision related to the normal procedure of two years' residence to be included on the waiting list. The housing manager Mr N Rees said that a number of people had come into the district in caravans and

were flooding the housing list. He said that it was obvious that the council could not give priority over 'the more genuine applicant'.

It was pointed out that if someone came into the district to work and took lodgings for two years, they would qualify, but if they took a caravan they would have to wait for five years. Caravan dwellers were simply not allowed the same rights as those who already lived in houses. Although there was increasing pressure on Travellers to give up the nomadic life and move into houses, this was a deliberate and overt attempt to make it harder for them to settle in Strood.

Panic was now spreading through the parishes around Cobham that the Travellers encamped on the verge of the A2 might end up on their own doorsteps and at a public meeting in Longfield in February 1962 local residents made it clear that they also did not want the Gypsies. Mr F T C Sims, a member of the parish and rural councils, explained the situation and added that, 'the gipsies have been on the A2 for a short time but the site is in a shocking condition. God forbid that we should ever have that in our parish...' He also issued a warning to the effect that, once a permanent site was established, not only the local Gypsies but also the Essex Gypsies and others from far away would come and camp there. Mr Sims said he knew of other sites, but as he did not want the Gypsies in Longfield, he 'would not wish them on anyone else.'

A letter to the *Gravesend Reporter*, 17 February 1962:

Sir,

These people are not the romantic gipsy type with violins around the camp fire in the evening. They are despised by the true gipsies and house dwellers alike for their mode of life. Take a look at the verge of the A2 after only two weeks of their occupation. Sentimentality is wasted on these people. They shirk the responsibility of living within the law in a civilised community and are quite happy and content to exist without paying rent, rates and income tax and take what they want without offering payment. The terror with which the parishioners of Darenth used to answer a knock on the door is now transferred to Stone. Respectable ladies insulted by obscenities and injured by stones thrown by the children of these so-called gipsies are afraid to complain because of the reprisals which will surely follow. It is not right to expect local authorities to assume responsibility and provide sites for this type of person, nor is it a national problem. We are dealing only with

The Ripley family settled into the new site at Cobham

a small community, which will not conform to ordinary decent rules of conduct and should be kept in order by applying existing laws. Apply the full powers of the Public Health Acts and the Caravan Sites Act and these people will either reform or vanish.

It was Norman Dodds who solved the immediate problem: he managed to procure a temporary site in Cobham and, with the goodwill of some locals and the hostility of a lot more, managed to provide pitches for a number of families. That he achieved this in the face of so much public opposition is testament to his tenacity: he described his appearance at a public meeting to discuss the proposed site as feeling like Daniel in the lions' den. When he stepped onto the platform it was several minutes before the shouts of abuse and threats of violence were quelled. Some local residents believed that the Gypsies would make their village dirty and objected to their children attending the village school; others feared petty pilfering and thieving, while one woman was afraid of being raped. Dodds admitted later that it was one of the most hostile and violent meetings he attended in his political career.

The new stopping place was on a disused and overgrown wartime gun site in Lodge Lane. Once permission had been granted by Sir Keith Joseph, Minister of Housing and Local

Joe and Genty Dennard with their friends on the Cobham site

Government, work began to make the six and a half acre site habitable. Several Traveller families, including the Bucknells, Chambers, Venners and Ripleys, joined with Norman Dodds to clear the brambles, lay hard standing, dig trenches for water supplies and restore toilet facilities in the old Nissen huts. In spite of pushing for longer, they were only granted permission for a two-year stay but during the appalling winter of 1962 fifty caravans pulled on.

Cobham was within the boundaries of Strood RDC and, in spite of the their previous attitude, they were eventually persuaded by Dodds' efforts and example to provide a permanent site in their borough. A small, disused caravan site already existed by the River Medway at Cuxton, tucked away in a fold of land and completely invisible from the road. It had originally been provided for construction workers building the M20 and was about three-quarters of a mile from the village. In Autumn 1963 twelve caravans from Lodge Lane pulled onto the site for the first time. It was a bold step by the council to allow its use

George Ripley remonstrates as the council prepare to pull them off the site at Cobham...

by Travellers, thus creating the very first municipal site for permanent occupation. This was achieved in spite of considerable opposition from Cuxton Parish Council who considered that because of the Gypsies' different mode of living 'a more remote site would be more suitable'. The families remaining on Cobham had won a temporary reprieve but inevitably the time soon came when their license to stay expired, and in spite of a request by Sir Keith Joseph that no action should be taken, the council's tractors were quickly back in action. This time the Travellers were put on a nearby piece of spare land owned by Lord Darnley, who soon obtained a court order against Strood Council. They were subsequently fined 350 guineas for trying to help the Gypsies who, after another inevitable eviction, ended up back on the verge of the A2.

We were on the Cobham site for two years. It was an army site for guns and there was a lot of concrete bunkers in there and all that and it was right in the middle of the fields. It was alright there, it was a good site, but it was only temporary. When the time was up they pulled people's trailers out and some of these had jacks down and people still had their china and bits and pieces up and a lot of it got broke and a lot of the caravans got broke. And what they done is, they didn't pull them into

…Eventually he has to stand by as they pull his trailer out

*Cobham Wood, they just pulled them alongside the road. Most people
hooked on and got into Cobham Woods themselves. Some people never
had vehicles and we tried to help one another, but they just pulled them
alongside the road and left them, and they separated them on different
parts of the roads from Cobham. We were there for a while then most
people made up their minds to move back onto the A2. There we were
summonsed every week, you got summonsed for stopping, summonsed
for your motor being there, whatever they could find to summons you
for, the police. That went on for years.*

Joe Ripley

It was simply no longer possible to find anywhere to stop. Legislation made roadside stopping difficult and local authorities
were rendering traditional stopping places inaccessible by dig-
ging ditches or building earth banks across them. The few
farmers or landowners that were prepared to offer winter stopping places in the corner of a field or in a wood were prevented from doing so by local councils enforcing the 1960 Caravan
Sites Act. In any case most Travellers had now replaced the old
wagons with motor-drawn trailers which were not suitable for
pulling across rough ground or into a wood. The old wagons
could be tucked into comparatively small spaces, they were
high off the ground and had large wheels and horses didn't get

Back on the side of the A2

stuck in mud like a motor vehicle would. The only option was to find a space on one of the dwindling pieces of waste ground or old rubbish tips, or to live on the wide grass verge of a main road.

The situation became particularly acute during the winter in those places that Travellers had traditionally resorted to around the fringes of London. They still needed to be close to large urban areas in order to find winter work but Belvedere Marsh, Corke's Meadow, Dartford Woods and the Cobham site had all closed and further down in Kent there was no longer any prospect of stopping around Ashford. Every autumn during the 1960s, the roadside verges around Orpington, Sidcup and the Crays began to fill with trailers and lorries as people sought somewhere to stop for the winter.

However, there were a few faint signs that a solution to the problem of stopping places was evolving. In the face of the usual predictable and vociferous opposition from nearby residents and a subsequent planning appeal, a twelve-pitch site was established in West Malling in 1964 and another on a disused rubbish tip at Edenbridge the following year. Together with the sites at Great Chart and Cuxton, Kent now boasted a grand total of forty-eight hard-won pitches – a beginning of sorts but it still hardly scratched the surface of what was required.

Under the M2 at Farthing Corner

There were still some places left that a trailer and lorry could pull onto. These tended to be parcels of waste ground or bomb sites which had been earmarked for development but on which building work had not yet begun. In 1965 several families had managed to pull onto a disused tip at the top of Star Lane in St Mary Cray and onto pieces of undeveloped building land in Court Road and Ramsden in Orpington. Others simply had to resort to the roadside verges and, during the mid-Sixties, strings of trailers became a familiar site alongside main roads. This was a miserable existence; it was dangerous for children to play outside and dogs had to be kept tied up. During the wet winter weather lorries pulling on and off the verges soon churned them into mud and there was the constant attention of the police and councils with their court orders to move on.

Half of the time the gavvers wouldn't let you stay anywhere anyway, they was hooking you on and moving you here, there and everywhere when we was smaller. Sometimes they used to make the boys move mother and us kids on, my brothers, because my father died when I was a little girl. But when the boys got old enough and they left home, my mum and my aunt Vi, when they had the trailers and the gavvers used to come, my mother, she used to give them the wheel brace and say, 'well, you tow them, you move them and wherever you move us, we're going to stop,' and that was that. Mother in the end always used to make the gavvers move us, but it didn't matter where you went, you was hunted anyway.'

Kay Smith

105

On the A21 at Badgers Mount

I remember the days when we were stopping along Badgers Mount, when we was taken to the court just for sawing off a limb from a tree and my dad was took to court for just pulling his vehicle up on the verge, doing criminal damage to the verge. I mean, he couldn't leave it in the middle of the road because another lorry could come along, or a car, and smash it to pieces, so he had to pull it somewhere didn't he? Like that there, they're saying criminal damage to the trees or to the fences or whatever, what else could they do? They had to keep warm in the winter, so that limb had to come off.

Bill Smith

In the face of public protest at the annual migration of Travellers into Orpington and St Mary Cray, Bromley Council formed a special committee in January 1966 to tackle the 'Gypsy problem' in the borough. Their remit was to examine the situation and to find some temporary sites while longer-term solutions to the problem of stopping places could be found. Alderman C L Smith was chair of the new committee and began his task with a positive outlook, although still with the now familiar aim of wanting to settle the Travellers into houses and integrate them into sedentary life. He was quoted in the *Kentish Times* of 7 January as saying:

The immediate aim was to fix up somewhere where they could spend a month or two without hindrance or annoyance. That would impose a considerable strain on a certain number of people, but he hoped that they would be inclined to give the Gypsies a chance. They were not nearly so bad as

Orpington & Kentish Times

INCORPORATING

ST. MARY CRAY, ST. PAUL'S CRAY, PETTS WOOD TIMES & WEST KENT MERCURY

TEL. ORPINGTON 25617   FRIDAY, FEBRUARY 17, 1967   Registered at General Post Office as a newspaper   LARGEST NETT SALE

Demonstrations against Council offer to gipsies

'KID-GLOVE' TREATMENT ANGERS RESIDENTS

Dramatic turn coolly received by spokesman

RESIDENTS over a wide area of Orpington, angered by what they call kid-glove tactics against gipsies, ended a week of mounting activity with a demonstration outside Bromley Town Hall, where the Council were meeting, on Monday.

About 100 of them, many carrying placards with anti-gipsy slogans on them, gathered at the main entrance, hoping to catch the eye of the Mayor and councillors. Most of these went in by a side door.

Police were at the entrance. About 20 minutes before the meeting was due to start the demonstrators—without placards—were allowed into the public gallery in the normal way.

A dramatic turn of events at the meeting (reported on Page 6) was the announcement that the gipsies had turned down the offer of a free, temporary site at Green-Street-Green, which the Special Committee had hoped would tempt them to move from the Court-road housing site and Star-lane tip.

It was this offer that had infuriated the residents and this news and the promise of stern, even drastic, action to move trespassers, did not please them entirely.

Said spokesman, Mr. John Hughes: "Retiring is the best

been representing the gipsies, told the *Kentish Times* that he hopes he and his friends on the Liaison Committee can help matters by bringing the two sides together. But the gipsies had to make the decisions for themselves.

He said Mr. Jack Dennard, spokesman for about 20 families at Court-road, had refused at a meeting with Council officials to inspect the site at Green-Street-Green.

"They decided not to go because there is no hard standing for the caravans, no toilets and no water supply. They also ... Grattan Puxon and Mr. Solly

NOVEL BID TO SWELL LEGION RANKS

OPERATION Super-charge, the British Legion's national campaign to boost membership, will be put into effect in a novel way by Orpington branch.

PRIORY OUTBUILDINGS MUST GO SAY COUNCIL

Little support for another deferment

Inside —

LABOUR DEMAND
ALL-IN SCHOOLS

PARKING AT

---

they were painted and, given a certain amount of help, there is no reason why, in a reasonably short time, these people cannot be rehabilitated and even at a later date, absorbed into the community.

Members of the committee visited the site at Cuxton and, in spite of the misgivings of inhabitants of the new houses on Ramsden Estate, provided the Travellers living on the land behind them with a temporary building housing a dozen chemical toilets. This new tolerance was not welcomed by many, fearing that it would attract other Travellers to the area once word got around. With nowhere else to stop, it was inevitable that this would happen and soon some families began arriving from Essex. However, all those that had arrived after 28 December 1966 were served notices to quit and those that remained were towed by the council onto the verge of Old Maidstone Road, Ruxley, just outside the borough.

Stopping on the old rubbish tip beside the A21 at Green Street Green

By February there were forty-six caravans in and around Orpington, mostly on the land at Court Road, Ramsden and Star Lane, St Mary Cray. Feelings were now running high: local houseowners were becoming angry at the council's apparent inability to move the Travellers on. They objected to the road-side verges being churned into mud, the noise of barking dogs, the piles of scrap that were accumulating outside their houses

Aerial view of Critall's Corner, Sidcup, 1967   Court Road, Orpington, early 1970s

and the acrid smoke from car body-shells being burnt out. Eventually, angered by what they described as the 'kid-glove' tactics being used against the Gypsies, a demonstration involving about a hundred people took place outside Bromley Town Hall where the council were meeting. The protesters were particularly upset that the council had offered the Travellers the use of an old rubbish tip at Green Street Green as a temporary stopping place. They feared that any lenience towards them would encourage others to come to Orpington, but they needn't have worried because the offer to stop at Green Street Green was turned down. Having looked at the site of the old tip, the Travellers decided not to risk pulling on because the ground was too soft and there was no hard standing. Nor was there any water or sanitation and it was next to a manhole which was opened daily for cesspool tankers to be emptied into. Having been turned down, the offer was immediately withdrawn and summonses issued to all caravan dwellers in the borough, including two who did subsequently pull on to the old tip.

Gillingham

By March work was underway on a new permanent site for twelve caravans at Star Lane and Bromley Council's special committee had a new chairman, Alderman H T Parkin, who, in common with his predecessor, continued to draw distinctions between the Travellers and 'real' Gypsies. He claimed that Bromley had done more for Travellers than other parts of the country and this was attracting even more of them to the borough. In mid-March the *Kentish Times* reported on a council meeting at which Alderman Parker was quoted as saying that their powers to move them on were limited:

> It is wise not to talk about these limitations openly, as the public and the press and then the Gypsies themselves become aware of the council's difficulties,' he said. Harassment might, in the Housing Minister's mind, refer to what the council were doing to these Travellers [who were not Gypsies]. But in his mind, harassment was what was being done to the residents by people who had no regard for the decencies of life.

Argument continued to rage in the letter columns of the *Orpington Times*, but not everyone was unsympathetic to the Travellers' plight. Several correspondents suggested that decent permanent sites be provided and one visited the temporary site at Star Lane. He reported that it was ankle-deep in mud and very noisy due to the proximity of the railway line. He also commented that, forty years ago, when he first came to Orpington, there were a lot more Gypsies around than now. He praised Gypsies for their family values, remarking that there was a lot that most people could learn from them. Needless to say, this prompted a predictably vitriolic reaction in the letter column the following week. Several people wrote defending the Travellers, including a Mr Richardson, but his suggestion that what was actually needed was some help prompted the inevitable retort the following week:

Letter to the Kentish Times, 18 August 1967

...Let us dispel the illusion that his friends are real gypsies and the romantic notion of the gentle traveller plying his trade from place to place by traditional means, disturbing nothing and nobody. The present settlers in this area have less justification for calling themselves gipsies than I have to claim Chinese nationality. It would be more correct to class these people under the general heading of unauthorised caravan dwellers. Mr Richardson's suggestion of discrimination is both irrelevant and misleading but deliberately inferred in order to create the impression that two species of people are involved, whereas the difference is a way of life that is irresponsible and anti-social...

By July the 'Gypsy problem' was as intractable as ever; the verges of main roads were still the only stopping places available and lines of caravans were strung along roadsides at Badgers Mount, Pratt's Bottom, Green Street Green and the Sidcup bypass. The new site at Star Lane was completed but remained unused until the Greater London Council, who owned the land, finally granted approval in September. Twelve families pulled on: each had their own amenity block with washrooms and toilets, there was hard standing on tarmac with plots that could be grassed or used however else the tenants wished. The following week the council turned up at the previously tolerated temporary site on the rubbish tip at Star Lane and, overseen by a force of fifty-two police officers, towed the remaining five caravans away to the roadside at Old Maidstone Road, Ruxley. This was the nearest roadside verge just outside the boundary of Bromley Borough. Speaking for the newly formed Gypsy Council, Gratton Puxon told the Kentish Times that the families had only been given ten minutes to pack and that damage had been done to the caravans and some crockery when they were towed away. Alderman Parkin replied in the same issue that, 'If people consistently refuse to go, we have the right to remove

Land earmarked for development behind the junction of Court Road and
the Highway, Orpington. Court orders were issued in February 1967
and by the end of March everyone had pulled off

them. If, in the process, they suffered damage, they must expect
it.' As soon as the caravans had gone, bulldozers moved in to
dig trenches and erect high banks of earth to prevent anyone
else from pulling on.

> When they says, 'Right, you're summonsed, you've got be taken to
> court,' the Travellers couldn't afford to pay for the fines. So what the
> Travellers used to do was to say, 'right, we'll move,' and some that didn't
> have vehicles to move their caravans, the council would come along and
> they'd move them. But where the council would move them, that was
> where they would stay until the next council came along and moved
> them again. But the ones that could move their own caravans along, OK,
> they'd move a couple of hundred yards or a mile down the road and say,
> 'Right, we've muvved, we're at a different spot.' But they'd do the same
> thing over and over again, they'd take more summonses out and say,
> 'well, you've got to move' and they'd push you from one area into
> another, to the boundary. They'd say, 'well, we want you out of our
> boundary,' — alright, we'll go into someone else's boundary, but when we
> get there, they want us out of there so where can we go, where do the
> Gypsies stop?
>
> Bill Smith

That same week court orders were served on families along
Court Road and at a meeting of the London Borough Association there were calls for the government to enact new 'get
tough' laws to deal with caravan dwellers who parked on road-
sides. Having provided sites for twelve caravans at Star Lane,
Bromley Council now felt justified in putting more pressure on
those who were living elsewhere in the borough. However, at
Bromley Magistrates Court in November an application by the
council to remove caravans at Pratts Bottom and Green Street
Green was adjourned so that magistrates could consider the
evidence. For the council, Mr Hepworth said they felt that they
had already done enough, but Mr Stephen Sedley, representing
the Travellers, submitted that the remaining twenty families had
nowhere else they could go: 'This is absolutely wrong, unjust
and something to which the Court should not be party. These
people are honest and decent. They have the social misfortune
of having nowhere to go.' He then quoted extracts from the
Declaration of Human Rights and handed a copy to the bench.
The magistrates postponed their decision until 11 December,
when they granted the council permission to remove the caravans. In the meantime others returning from the summer's
work continued to arrive, looking for stopping places.
Sevenoaks District Council began to worry that if things were
made more difficult for Travellers in Bromley they would move
southwards into their area. One council member also asserted
that Gypsies were 'pouring through Dartford Tunnel saying
"Kent's the place for us".'

In 1965 the government commissioned a national survey of
Travellers and their living conditions. The results were published in 1967 in a report entitled 'Gypsies and other Travellers'. It concluded that sixty per cent of the families surveyed
had travelled in the previous year but mainly because they had
been forced to do so by councils and police. Only a third of
them had access to a water supply or rubbish disposal and very
few of their children received any schooling. The stringent
planning controls introduced in the 1960 Caravan Sites Act had
made the situation worse, forcing many families to leave unofficial sites and go back on the road to live in very poor conditions. None of this cut any ice with the *Orpington and Kentish Times*:

Editorial Comment, 3 November 1967

The main theme of this report is sympathetic to the gypsies,
reminding the public of the 'remarkable fact that for most

West Malling

travelling families there is nowhere they can legally put their home; they are within the law only when they are moving along the road'. Residents of Bromley Borough and the Orpington district particularly will be forgiving for commenting that the really remarkable fact about the paragraph is that it does not deter any gypsies from stopping here. Then the suggestion that not all of the complaints of the settled population against gipsies, despoiling the countryside, fear of criminal acts, public health hazards and the feeling that gipsies are social parasites are well grounded and the necessity of breaking down the general hostility towards gipsies. What do those who have had to put up with gipsies on their boundaries in the Court Road, St Mary Cray, Green Street Green and Pratt's Bottom areas have to say about that? In a borough where they provide from the rates a place for gipsies, too. For government departments to go prattling on like this and do nothing positive to ensure that the matter is dealt with on a national basis or giving local authorities precise powers to deal with the situation in their own borders is infuriating. It seems to be more of a crime to be 'members of the settled population' than it is to be a gipsy.

Years ago, when they were in trailers stopping alongside the road, we used to have people what we used to call 'petrol bombers', we'd have people come along in cars giving a lot of abusive language, hollering out 'Gypsies, pikies'. Some nights we'd only have candlelight, we'd have nothing to run no electric lights, by night time we used to get some come along on motorbikes or in cars, chuck bricks or bits of iron or something like that. But when you get someone come along and they're filling a bottle up or a can with petrol and they're putting a piece of rag into it and they're flinging it at you to set you alight, the kids was very frightened and scared. I can remember myself being frightened and scared as a little boy and nobody knows the fear until it happens to them. But when things did happen like that, some of the Gypsies used to retaliate. They used to stay back in the hedges or lay down alongside the caravan and wait and try and stop the car or take the car number to report it. But it went on and on like that until the Gypsies used to retaliate by shooting the side of the car with a catapult or slingshot. That was only protecting their own self, that's better than standing still or laying still and waiting for something to come through a window full of petrol to set everybody alight.

Bill Smith

The late 1960s and early 1970s represent one of the lowest points in recent Gypsy history. By this time the seasonal farm work had all but disappeared and agriculture had become highly industrialised. The last farm to pick hops by hand finally mechanised in 1969 and farmers were now employing students for what little hand-picking work remained. The demand for wooden clothes pegs had been overtaken by mass-produced versions and other traditional woodland craft products like primrose baskets and wooden flowers had fallen out of favour in modern, sophisticated households. Places to stop were becoming virtually impossible to find; the disappearance of farm work and the rigid application of the 1960 Caravan Sites Act had meant the disappearance of somewhere to live for half the year.

Of course local house dwellers objected to the piles of scrap and dismantled motor cars that lay around the trailers on road-sides but neither did the Travellers desire to live like that. With virtually no other work available and nowhere else to stop, it was sheer force of circumstance that drove them to scratch an income in this way. Traditionally literacy was not part of the education that was received on the road from parents and grandparents. Practical farm skills, being able to catch rabbits

Scads Hill, Chislehurst Road, Orpington in March 1968. The site of a
derelict nursery awaiting development provided another temporary
stopping place

and hedgehogs, to prepare and cook them with wild plants, to
breed, break and drive horses and the ability to skilfully work
wood and metal with improvised tools all count for nothing
when living in a trailer on a suburban roadside. The conven-
tional Gorjer workplace was not an option for the independ-
ent-minded, self-determining Traveller who had never been to
school and couldn't read or write. In any case, the chances of
getting permanent employment as a Gypsy whose address was
a caravan on the roadside were non-existent. Neither was it
much use knocking on the doors of hostile local house
dwellers who felt that by not giving you temporary employment in the form of odd jobs such as tree pruning they would
encourage you to move on.

In a period of about twenty-five years the traditional
nomadic existence that had changed little for generations had
been systematically dismantled and the Traveller population left
to fend for itself in alien circumstances as best it could. This

enforced change of lifestyle had far-reaching repercussions that might not have been anticipated at the time but which are obvious in retrospect. Many Travellers who were themselves born on the roadside in bender tents or alongside horse-drawn wagons, following an ancient and simple pattern of existence, now found that their existing life skills and knowledge were redundant. They were also faced with the task of bringing up their own children in radically different circumstances from those that they had known and grown up in themselves. Living in a trailer on a piece of waste ground surrounded by scrap and burnt-out motor cars doesn't afford the same opportunities for children to play as the woods and fields of the open country.

Change was inevitable as Travellers faced being forced onto claustrophobic permanent sites with all their rents and regulations. Living on a council site was anathema to the Gypsy way of life, even though most had by now come to the conclusion that even that was preferable to the difficulty of surviving on the roadside. Pitches on sites were, and to this day remain, at a premium, forcing many Travellers to seriously consider moving into houses. They had always lived separately from the Gorjer but were now under immense pressure to give up their caravan homes and move in next door to them. Life on the road always affords the opportunity to escape hostility and persecution by moving on, but when finally the pressure is to stay put, it poses new problems of integration for both the Traveller and the non-Traveller. The house dwellers who didn't want Gypsies on roadsides or on sites nearby certainly didn't want them living next door. For many Traveller families, moving into a house for the first time is a step into the unknown. For people who have always been sheltered by bricks and mortar it is difficult to understand the trauma that this apparently simple transition can cause the Traveller. Coupled with the pressures to conform to a Gorjer way of life, it represents the final renunciation of all that defines their identity as Gypsy or Traveller. For many Travellers, being forced to live in a house and adopt the lifestyle of those who have destroyed yours is the final humiliation.

CHAPTER FIVE

After the Act

F ollowing the untimely death in 1965 of Norman Dodds, the MP who had done so much in Parliament to raise awareness of the problems of Travellers, it was the liberal MP for Orpington, Eric Lubbock (now Lord Avebury) who took up their cause. In 1967 he promoted a private member's bill to deal with the dubious practices of some owners of mobile-home sites. In response to the findings of the 1967 report 'Gypsies and other Travellers', the government offered to support his bill if he included a second part dealing with the provision of Gypsy sites.

The resulting 1968 Caravan Sites Act was supposed to bring some relief to the situation and although the act placed a duty upon local authorities to provide sites for Gypsies 'residing in

Beside the A21 at Polhill, after many years of toleration a permanent site was eventually built on the spot

Harrow Manor Way, Abbey Wood, 1970s

or resorting to their area', local opposition to proposed sites was always fierce. In order to help persuade councils and those who elected them to accept the requirements of the act a sweetener was offered in the form of 'designation'. Local authorities were required to make regular counts of Travellers in their area, and once they were deemed to have provided sufficient pitches they were then allowed to have their area 'designated', which automatically made unauthorised stopping a criminal offence. This theoretically made the eviction and moving on of anyone camped on the roadside much easier and quicker. However, with the certain knowledge that the electorate would take a dim view of their local authorities providing permanent sites, heels were dragged.

The act was seriously flawed because no time limit for compliance was built into it and by 1994 when it was finally repealed many local authorities had still not fulfilled their legal obligation to Travellers. In addition, London boroughs were only required to provide fifteen pitches, regardless of the number of Travellers in their localities. The other local authorities were certainly not over-eager to make accurate counts of Gypsies in their areas; every site that was proposed immediately became a planning and political nightmare so inevitably the surveys that were undertaken grossly underestimated the numbers. Residents' associations and local papers were guaranteed

GYPSIES
DO WE WANT THEM?
IF YOU CARE ABOUT KEMSING
PROTEST
PUBLIC MEETING
ST EDITHS HALL
16 MARCH 7.30p.m.
CONFRONT K.C.C.

A concerted campaign was mounted against a site which was proposed for derelict land next to Kemsing Station

to create a storm of protest against any attempt to 'dump Gypsies and Travellers in their backyards'.

For the purpose of the act it was necessary to identify those who were eligible for sites, resulting in an inevitable return to the age-old discussion of who was, and who was not, a 'real Gypsy'. It included 'Persons of nomadic habit of life, whatever their race or origin', but went on to specifically exclude travelling showmen and circus people. In spite of the 1968 Act, provision was appallingly slow. Whenever a council investigated suitable sites, local residents and parish councils would erupt in a fury of objection.

In 1967 Maidstone Borough Council built sites at Ulcombe and Stilebridge, providing another twenty-seven pitches and Dartford built a twelve-pitch site in Dartford Woods at Bean in 1969. This brought the total number of pitches in the county to ninety-two, but it took another five years before this was increased to ninety-six with an expansion of the West Malling site. The rate of provision was appallingly slow as the provision of each new site, or the expansion of an existing one, had to be fought for every inch of the way. It wasn't just members of the public who objected to the location of new sites: their fears and worries were fuelled by those who should have known better. In 1963 an enquiry took place into proposals for a site at Stilebridge, in the Maidstone constituency of the Conservative MP John Wells. It was probably this event which prompted him to introduce the Gipsy Camps (Compensation) Bill in the House of Commons in the same year which would provide compensation for owners of property near to 'Gipsy camps' that were provided or controlled by local authorities. His stated aim was to 'enable local authorities to proceed even more willingly and rapidly towards the establishment of these important camps'. He suggested that compensation should be paid for damage to land, buildings, crops and other vegetation, chattels and livestock in the vicinity of the new site. Although he claimed his intention was to speed up the process of provision, his words clearly sent out a message that Gypsies

Site building at Stilebridge near Marden

would cause damage in the locality. Some simple research would quickly have informed him that there had been no such instances of criminal behaviour or damage arising from the sites that had already been provided at Great Chart and Cobham. Thus it was purely personal opinion borne out of pre-conceptions rather than hard facts that motivated his proposed bill, which assumed the worst and reinforced prejudice rather than defusing it. Mr Wells' bill got no further than its first reading but it clearly illustrated public attitudes towards site provision. Against this background of opposition, the slow process of provision then came to a total halt in the county for seven long years until another site was opened, this time providing sixteen pitches at Vauxhall on the outskirts of Canterbury, the first in East Kent.

By the early 1970s the traditional stopping places had all but disappeared and post-war rebuilding had finally reclaimed the bomb sites and waste ground that had offered temporary places of respite from roadside harassment. The County Council was actively scrutinising every patch of waste ground in Kent in the search for suitable sites. District and parish councils remained vigilant and as soon as they got wind that the county was looking at a piece of land on their patch, their defences would swing into action. In spite of large numbers of Travellers in East Kent, the only provision in the area was the site at Vauxhall, with the result that there was considerable unauthorised

Dark Farm near Borough Green, 1970s

stopping in the area around Canterbury. One such place was the pit village of Woolage where the National Coal Board and the district council began eviction proceedings against three Traveller families after local villagers threatened to 'take the law into their own hands'. 'The villagers are absolutely fed up with these people,' Councillor Elijah Heathcote told his council in August 1970. 'There was a move to get up a gang to go down to the caravan site only last night. I have lived in the village all my life but have never known a feeling like this. I do not know how much longer I can keep the village in check.' Councillor Heathcote said villagers had had the problem for four months and had had enough. 'We are mainly miners and farmers trying to maintain decent standards. They use the woods as a toilet so that village people cannot now walk there or allow their children to play there. The smell from the site is appalling, it is buzzing with flies and we fear there will be an outbreak of typhoid or some similar disease. A farmer put a trough in his field for his cows to drink from. This is now the main water supply. Not only that, they bathe in it and even bring their washing to it. They are scavengers and parasites who live off rubbish and filth.' Following this report in the local paper, a member of the local Gypsy support group visited the site and reported that, 'We found a small neat encampment; the caravans were spotlessly maintained within and outside the camp site was tidy. There were no smells or flies and the typhoid that one councillor had feared seemed impossible. As regards the

Stopping in Staplehurst

water supply, the Travellers claim to be provided from a local garage.' He went on to say that the Travellers would willingly pay rent and rates on a permanent site if one were available. They were earning good money by tarmacking and landscape gardening but had found that their normal sites were now subject to legal restrictions.

The situation at Woolage was typical, there were simply not enough places on official sites for those who wanted them and the search for somewhere to stop was becoming increasingly desperate. Any land that was apparently unused or semi-derelict and not protected by ditches or banks was likely to be taken over as word got round. One such place was a disused army camp in Headcorn Road, Staplehurst. The first Travellers pulled

The old army camp at Staplehurst

on in 1972 and within a year there were a hundred caravans on the site. It was a desolate place with no water, sanitation or refuse collection but at least it was somewhere to stay. The council were unable to bring legal action to clear the site because they were having problems identifying the owner. It had originally belonged to Joe Sorrell, a local farmer, but after his death his will had been contested and until a high court hearing could take place to establish who owned the land Maidstone Rural Council had to drop their eviction proceedings. This inevitably caused much annoyance to local residents who wanted the Travellers moved off as quickly as possible.

In 1974 the police carried out a massive raid on the site. At dawn on 1 February, 150 officers sealed it off by blocking the entrance with cars. A mobile headquarters was parked in the centre of the camp and every caravan was searched over a three-hour period. Despite their best efforts, out of a population of at least three hundred people only two men were taken away for questioning (one was later released without charge, the other was later released on bail pending further enquiries).

Swan Farm, New Ash Green

This was a large-scale operation in which a hundred homes were searched but nothing was found. An equivalent operation that targeted a hundred neighbouring houses and sealed off a whole street is very difficult to imagine; easier to comprehend would be the public outcry if such action was undertaken. To inconvenience such a large number of people with no demonstrable outcome must mean that either the intelligence was very flawed or that it was simply an attempt to intimidate the Travellers.

Although the police had the resources to pull together enough numbers to make their presence felt, the size of the camp was a deterrent to any aggravation that members of the general public might attempt to cause. Eventually it was the Travellers themselves who resolved the situation for the locals: as the annual round of summer work began they started to move off. As soon as the last trailer had left in June a digger was hastily drafted in and earth banks were thrown up around the site.

Meanwhile, at Swan Farm at Ash near Hartley another unof-

Eviction from land behind the industrial estate at Parkwood, Maidstone

ficial site was evolving. In 1974 some land on the farm had been acquired by an Essex-based firm who were selling 'leisure plots' to Travellers at £450 each. At the other end of the county a similar situation was developing where a local man was also selling plots of land to Travellers at Yorkletts near Whitstable. Neither of these sites had planning permission for permanent residence but, with nowhere else to stop, Travellers took the risk of handing over their money and pulling on. These unofficial private sites did alleviate the problem to some extent but the shortage of council sites remained acute and many families were still left with nowhere to go.

Even though life on a permanent site was anathema to most Travellers, it was reluctantly accepted as better than being on the verges of main roads. Being exposed to harassment from the police, local authorities and passing motorists as well as to the dangers of passing traffic was an unpleasant existence. Although invisibility had always been a way of avoiding harassment, it also undermined the Travellers' argument for more sites. When the majority of the Gypsy population tucked themselves away from the public eye, their numbers appeared to be far less than was actually the case, thus seeming to confirm council surveys with their low figures. Reluctantly, many decided to adopt the high-profile tactics that Norman Dodds had

Joe Ripley

first introduced them to when they remained on the verges of the A2 after being pulled from Dartford Woods. Although being so visible was new and uncomfortable to the Travellers, it was one way of revealing their plight: sooner or later pressure would be applied by the local housed population for places to be provided for Travellers to live out of sight.

> Travellers in the old days would find the loneliest place they could find when they were travelling about with a horse and wagons to pull. The kids couldn't go to school because the police would move them on every other day, so if they got a week in place they were lucky. So they'd find a lonely old place in the middle of the woods, the lonelier the better. But once they started building sites, then people pulled out more in the open so that they would stand a better chance of getting a site built.
>
> Joe Ripley

Pulling on to a council site for the first time was taking a big step into the unknown. Until then Travellers had had the freedom to come and go as they pleased. Even though the places to stop had been vanishing, there had still been a measure of self-determination. At least there had been the feeling that the open road was still ahead, that you were mobile; even if you didn't move, you knew that you could if you wanted to.

The designers and planners of council sites had no knowledge or understanding of Traveller culture and lifestyle, or if they did they chose to disregard it. The sites were designed and built more like holiday caravan parks than places of permanent occupation by people who were mainly self-employed. In the 1960s and 70s many Travellers were earning a living by collecting, sorting and selling scrap metal. This was not allowed on the sites and so nowhere was provided to do it. There was little storage space for materials or tools and the carrying out of work such as car repairs was also forbidden. Life on the council sites was hedged about with rules which council officials had to attempt to enforce. The keeping of pets was not usually allowed in spite of the fact that dogs had long been an intrinsic part of Gypsy life, used to hunt for food, as guard dogs or simply for company; chickens and game birds had also commonly been kept, even on the road. Outside fires, once the all-important communal focal point, were also forbidden. All of these imposed restrictions seemed pointless and merely added insult to injury.

Such was the demand for places on sites that anyone who vacated their pitch stood to lose it. Councils would only allow

Star Lane Site, St Mary Cray, 1980s

tenants to be absent for a limited period, usually a few weeks, after which it was assumed that the tenancy was forfeited. Even if the council didn't take the pitch back it was highly likely that someone else would simply pull on, with or without permission. This precluded families from pulling off to live and work on farms for a season or simply going off travelling for a month or two in the summer – to do so could mean that you would end up back on a muddy roadside verge the following winter. In short, many of those things that most Travellers considered intrinsic to their lifestyle had to be forfeited in order to remain on a site which they didn't want to be on in the first place.

Not only were the rules oppressive but the overall design of the sites left a lot to be desired. When stopping on a farm or other patch of land, caravans could be organised in family groups and arranged to respect one another's privacy. On a site the pitches were usually laid out in rows alongside an access road and there was often no choice where the caravans were to be positioned. Not only were they much closer than people were used to but frequently the windows lined up alongside

Minnie and Rose Ripley, Star Lane Site

each other, maybe only a few feet away. This confinement brought tensions, particularly if you happened to end up next to a family that you didn't get on with. On the road there was always the opportunity to move on if there was friction, but on a site you were stuck with each other. These problems only served to heighten the overall feeling of claustrophobia and resentment of a system that had destroyed a way of life, herding everyone into what could feel like a concentration camp.

> *If my father was alive, I don't think he would ever live on a site because he liked his fire too much, he liked being out round the fire. That was his way of life and, on a site, you can't have a fire. You see, cooking on a gas with saucepans and that, that wasn't the way that I was fotch up. I was fotch up round a fire, having my food round a fire. The sites today is slowly doing away with Travellers. They won't die out altogether but sites are changing the way of life. Nine Travellers out of ten, their kids*

Eviction from land at Church Farm, Milton near Sittingbourne in 1982. Although the number of pitches on council sites in Kent had risen to 230, unauthorised encampments were still commonplace. This was thirteen years after the 1968 Act requiring local authorities to provide sites for all Gypsies 'residing in or resorting to' their area

are brought up in a Gorjer's world, a Gorjer's way of life. I think that if their mums and dads had a choice, their kids wouldn't have been brought up like that.

Minnie Ripley

The construction of permanent sites slowly continued in spite of the fact that they were an imperfect solution. Travellers felt that the very idea of being forcibly restricted went against everything they held dear whilst local residents didn't want Gypsies permanently in their area, so no one was happy. In the mid 1970s there was still a serious lack of provision, particularly in the Dover area where several families had been stopping around Aylesham. In spite of the obvious need, it took a full five years to establish a site there due to the consistent opposition of local residents. At a parish council meeting reported in the *Kentish Express* in September 1976, Councillor Derek Garrity of Aylesham Parish Council protested, 'This parish is ringed by Gypsies. Years ago we used to have them here for a couple of weeks and then they went. Now we feel these people are being forced on us. I want to know if this area is being used as a dumping ground for Gypsies.' In January 1977 the newspaper reported that the village had 'lost another round in its battle to keep Gypsies out of the village,' when a

Church Marsh, Sittingbourne

joint council committee recommended acceptance of the plans. Councillor Mrs Leith said Aylesham Parish Council had very strong objections to the site. Every householder in Ackholt had signed a petition, 'but if there is anything no one wants, then they say, dump it in Aylesham.' Another article in the same edition of the paper described objections from other quarters:

The National Union of Mineworkers, also concerned about the project says, 'Aylesham has been treated without compassion by Dover Council'. Other objections have also come from the National Association of Colliery Overmen, Deputies and Shotfirers, Snowdown Recreation and Playing Field Association, Snowdown Working Men's Club and Institute – who say the gipsies are a nuisance in clubs.

The arguments rolled on and the plans finally went to a public inquiry in 1979 where local residents offered a stream of objections. These included the noise of children playing on the site, the fact that permanent sites were unnecessary because Gypsies were nomadic people, and that it was adding insult to injury to put what was likely to be an 'offensive and smelly' site next to a residential area. Finally, just as the site was about to be

A new site under construction at Ruxley in
1990 to provide places for families still living
on the old tip at Green St Green. It is lined by an
8 foot high concrete wall and is a few feet away
from a busy dual carriageway, resulting in high
levels of noise and atmospheric pollution

built in 1980 and in spite of the fact that
there were unauthorised encampments in
the area, the parish council suggested that
it was a waste of money and that 'it could
make a saving which could probably be
spent on something else'. In spite of all
the delays and fuss the site finally opened
in 1981, offering another sixteen pitches.

The inevitable public outcry that arose
whenever a new site was proposed meant
that the choice of location was severely
limited. Invisibility became one of the
main factors that determined where a site
might be built. They were usually on the
very outskirts of towns on land that no
one else wanted. The Edenbridge site was
on an old rubbish dump and the site at
North Farm in Tunbridge Wells was sand-
wiched between an open municipal rubbish tip and the sewage treatment works
(the smell was appalling and changed
depending on which way the wind was
blowing on any particular day). The site
had been built very cheaply and, shortly

Joe Jones looks at a site nearing completion at
Murston, near Sittingbourne in 1990. The road
to the entrance gate (above) is lined with a
barbed-wire fence; the crooks at the top of the
posts are facing towards the road to keep people
from climbing into the neighbouring land. The
need to surround the site with an eight-foot-
high barbed-wire-topped fence is in itself ques-
tionable. The fact that the posts around it are
facing inwards infers that they are to keep the
new residents in

after it was occupied, the caravans began to sink into the surface. The road quickly became potholed, there was no electricity and only portable lavatories which continuously froze or flooded. The Cuxton site lay well out of sight on the banks of the Medway between a sewage treatment works, an old brickfield being used as a refuse tip and a railway line. The Bean site was constructed in an old clay pit in a wood miles from anywhere and Denton in Gravesend was built on what turned out to be contaminated industrial land on the Thameside marshes. When there was any chance of a site being visible, either from neighbouring houses or just a road, it was 'screened' by a concrete fence or high earth mounds. Not only were the caravans invisible to the outside world, but the outside world was invisible from the caravans. When the site was in a remote location a high wire fence replaced the screening: you could have a view but only through wire mesh topped with barbed wire. Having had their nomadic way of life destroyed, the site designs and choices of location further reinforced the Travellers' sense of being hemmed in.

> These sites what they made, with all fences and all barbed wire round them, they're really putting the Gypsies down, because the caravan sites are like concentration camps, that's what I can picture them by anyway. Wire-mesh fencing all the way round and about three strands of barbed wire on the top, going all the way round. These private holiday caravan sites that people own up and down the country, there's one down the road here, Woodlands — can't see no barbed-wire fences all round them, and it's not closed in and it's absolutely done out lovely, properly as a caravan site should be done. But these Gypsy caravan sites, to be quite honest, I wouldn't stop on them.
>
> Jack Hilden

> They put barbed-wire fences all the way around them, or a big high brick wall. That's no way of life to live for the Gypsies. I mean, Travellers are used to freedom, aren't they? To look across and they can see the meadows, the fields or whatever. It's either that or be summonsed every day along of the roadside and being pulled from one place to another and in one court after another.
>
> Bill Smith

> They cut your friends off, they cut your way of life off and you're basically tied down to one place and really and truly I wonder who did win the war. Was it Hitler? Because we're on a concentration camp now, we

Cherry picking, Pembury near Tunbridge Wells. Every summer the whole
family pulls into the orchard to pick the fruit which is then sold on
roadside stalls. The children leave school before the end of the summer
term so that the three generations remain together for the duration of
the summer

> got barbed wire around us, we've got fences around us and we're put
> miles from anywhere. We've got a big river down the bottom of the
> road there, three lakes if we want to go and do away with ourselves,
> because this is the ideal place to be depressed – here.
>
> Albert Scamp (on Murston site)

Traditionally, the extended family has been central to Gypsy
life. The culture had little or no investment in either the permanence of material possessions or a fixed home; it relied instead
on relationships, particularly those within the family, to provide a sense of belonging and security. Brothers, sisters, aunts,
uncles, parents and grandparents stayed together as a self-sufficient unit of mutual support. If the outside world as it passed
by was an ever-changing place, then continuity was found
within the family.

As well as being an emotional stronghold, the family unit is
also a practical one in which skills, finances and feelings are

Hop training at Sutton near Maidstone

(opposite) Bill Smith, Rose Ripley and Jez Smith

shared. This all-important interdependence within the extended family was also jeopardised by life on the permanent sites. Pitches only tended to become vacant one at a time, so if a couple did manage to get a place it was unlikely that their parents or brothers and sisters would also manage to get onto the same site. Many Travellers still lived in the traditional trailer, which only had one large room – the beds pulled out from beneath the bench seats or folded down from cupboards. Thus at night the trailer was transformed into a bedroom and as the children grew older, they would in turn move out into a trailer of their own. If you lived on a council site this was not always possible: not only was there insufficient space to keep bringing additional trailers onto a pitch, but most sites only allowed a maximum of two per pitch. In practice Travellers on sites were being penalised for having children, and the situation would only get worse when eventually the offspring would also find partners and want to start families of their own. Travellers traditionally start their families at a younger age than non-Travellers, with childcare and support being shared across several generations as sons work alongside their fathers and mothers and daughters share domestic work. The tightly knit extended family unit works both ways: it provides childcare for the young and looks after its old people who in return supply the wisdom of age and play an active part in looking after their grandchildren while parents are working. Nursing homes or hospitalisation had never been an option on the road; as the elderly became increasingly frail they remained in the twenty-four hour care of the younger family members. To settle on a site meant not only the rejection of all that defined you as Gypsy, it also required the break-up of your family.

Years ago the way of Travellers, if they had a father, mother or whatever and they got old, they still stayed with the younger generation until they passed away, they died. They stayed together and that went on and on.

Albert Scamp and his wife with Joe Jones on Church Marsh, 1990

Today, I've got sons and daughters of my own, I'm on a site now and I've only got one pitch, one bay and I'm only allowed to have one caravan on there. So what happens when my daughter gets married? She can't stay on my plot because I've only got the one plot for my caravan, probably on his [daughter's prospective husband], the same with him. So where do they go, where do they end up at? I mean, Travellers should stay together and I would like, if my daughters got married or my son, I would like for them to stay as close as possible. That's the way of Travellers years and years back, they stayed together, you know, family, uncles, brothers, sisters, whatever — they stayed together. But today, Travellers, they're parted up. You got one site in Orpington, you've got another site down in Sittingbourne. I've got family on Sittingbourne and I've got family on Orpington, so before I can see them I've got to travel down there.

Bill Smith

Once a pitch had been secured on a council site it was possible to keep an ear to the ground and find out in advance if any

Albert Scamp

other places on the site were likely to become vacant. Over the years many did manage to take on neighbouring pitches for children or parents and engineer the situation whereby the extended family could once again be together. However, the chronic shortage of pitches meant that not everyone could work the system in this way and there was an inevitable and increasing drift into nearby housing. Some Gypsies and Travellers have always taken this option and settled down in one place, either in a house or in a caravan on a piece of land, but now there was no longer any choice in the matter as children grew up and started their own families. The desire was usually still to remain as close as possible to at least one set of parents, so particular areas of council-house estates near to sites or traditional stopping places gradually became populated by Travellers. This had already begun to happen in St Mary Cray after Corke's Meadow was closed and also at Belvedere and Abbey Wood after the flooding of the marshes. There was a similar pattern in Luton in the Medway towns near to Ash Tree Lane,

Nelson Duval stopping at Collier Street for Horsemonden Fair, 1995

which had long been a stopping place, as well as in areas of Gravesend and Sittingbourne near to the marshes.

> *We travelled around, mostly on farms in the summer, and through the winter time we used to go back in a house. When I was young, there were no permanent sites so it got so hard that my mum had to go in a*

house in the winter. There was nowhere to pull, there was no running
water, no electricity and obviously my mum and dad had to live. They
couldn't take us to work with them so we were put into schools and
they went in a house.

Albert Scamp

Having had the Travelling life destroyed by the Gorjer, being
forced into a house to live like one can be a devastating experience. Despite the fact that houses are more spacious, many
Travellers feel oppressed and claustrophobic within brick walls.
A trailer responds to the weather, it rocks in the wind, you can
hear rain falling on the roof and there is still a sense of being
close to nature and the elements. Houses cosset their occupants, insulating them from the sounds, smells and feelings of
the outdoors.

> A house to a Traveller is a prison. There's no way that a Traveller likes to
> be closed in. Their way of life is travelling, along of the countryside. I
> had to go in a house, the caravan was going to be impounded and taken
> away. They said the kids could even be taken away from me and put
> away in a home, I mean, I don't want to lose all my family. If they're
> going to take the Gypsy life away from me, I don't want them to take
> my wife, kids, brother and sisters away. I had the choice of going in, but
> I was only in there for about a month and I was back out into a cara-
> van. At least I did go in and tried, but after the try it was no good and I
> came back in the caravan to live, and I'm still in one today.

Bill Smith

During the day, in contrast to the quiet, sterile emptiness of a
suburban street, Gypsy sites are busy places. With most people
working on an ad hoc, self-employed or casual basis, there are
always comings and goings, maybe business transactions or
just friends and family dropping in for a visit. Because there are
always friendly people about it is safe for children to play outside and to have the run of the site, interacting with other families. Once housed, there is danger on the street from cars or
from other children who may choose to gang up on young
Travellers.

> You'd be better off in a house, wouldn't you, because you've got every-
> thing to your hand, you've got your water, your toilet, your baths, every-
> thing. Ain't got that here, so if it comes to it, I suppose, yes, we'd go, but
> all the time we could get on a site and have our own vans like we are,
> we'd sooner do that. That's what we've been used to, but if it come to it
> and they said there's nowhere else to go, I suppose we'd go in. Perhaps

141

Louie Cooper on Swan
Farm, Ash, 1998

we'd get used to it, I don't know. It would be different wouldn't it? It would be different, really, but I suppose we'd have to get used to it if there wasn't anywhere else to go. It's just that you can't see all your own friends around you, all your own Travellers, if you're in a house, can you? Just locked in, really, aren't you, behind walls? Gorjers all been brought up in them houses, from babies, they're all used to it, but all the Travellers ain't.

Louie Cooper

Although sites were an imperfect solution, life on them still retained some of the flavour of the old ways. The old traditional stopping places were inhabited only by Travellers. If other people did live there then they would have to conform to the dominant Traveller culture and not vice versa. Codes of behaviour and mutual understandings were shared and accepted. On a council site the same holds true as the Travellers are still amongst their own, but those who by force of circumstance become physically separated from the Traveller community can experience feelings of profound alienation.

We were up Seven Mile Lane, on that piece of ground – they were putting a road through there anyway so we had to get off. Then I went in hospital for the baby and it was either coming out with a small, new baby onto the roadside with no water, or moving into a flat. So I stuck into the hospital until I got a flat – which I did, up Parkwood. I hated it at first, but I had the little baby anyway, Emma, so obviously I got used to it. I was there about two and a half years. Then from there I went into a house and that was even worse. I hated upstairs. I would have moved into a tent if I had to, to get out of it, I hated it there. I cried nearly every day.

Kay Smith

She's never lived in a house before, my wife, and I have so I knew what I was expecting. Me and her was having more rows in a house than we were in a van because it's not our way of life. She couldn't buckle down to the life of a Gorjer, we were so used to the travelling life. If we had to get off this site and they said you'd have to take a house, I'd hitch this van up and I'd be off here today and I'd travel every roadside before I'd take a house. Because the houses, they're alright for those who've been brought up to know the Gorjer way. Why should we give our culture up to live their way of life? It's like asking a black man to be white, you can't do that.

Albert Scamp

143

Kay Smith

Moving on has always been an immediate and practical way of putting a physical distance between yourself and those that you don't get on with, but once in a house life takes on greater inertia and it is not possible to move anywhere at short notice. Even on a site your home still has wheels, even if they haven't turned for years, but moving house entails a lengthy process of finding new tenants or purchasers as well as somewhere else to live. When the neighbours resent having Gypsies next door and make life difficult, the inability to move increases the feelings of imprisonment and oppression that house-dwelling already causes.

> I had a nice house, it was brand new, but we had that much opposition
> from people and prejudice saying what they viewed through the past
> history about Gypsies. We went away [fruit picking] and when we
> came back the house was smashed up — because travelling people always
> go away in the summer. When we came back it was smashed up, there
> was Gypsies [painted] on the wall. We had residents' committees up, we
> had the lot up against us, so I just had to give the key back in to the
> council because I couldn't put up with it.
>
> Albert Scamp

> What they're trying to do is get rid of Gypsies completely. They say, 'If
> we get them out of caravans, off them sites, put them in houses, we can
> say that's the end of the Gyspies'. But it's not, they've still got the Gyp-
> sies in houses. I know a street now where there are Gypsies in houses
> and the Gorjers have moved away just because they know that a Gypsy
> is based next to them. When they find out, 'Oh, my next door neighbour
> is a Gypsy', their friends say, 'Oh, you're stopping with the Gypsies,
> aren't you frightened you're going to get fleas from the Gypsies or some
> sort of disease?'
>
> Bill Smith

It used to be said that a Gypsy could never own more than a horse could pull: there was only a limited amount of space in a wagon or caravan so very little that wasn't absolutely necessary for survival could be kept. Once settled in a house with more space available, the physical baggage of life inevitably increases, more belongings are accumulated and, gradually, the anchoring weight of possessions makes moving on a less appealing prospect. The house itself is also a burden: caravan-living is comparatively cheap and simple with no bills to pay, only a small space to heat and light; very little maintenance is necessary, furnishings are few and are all built in. House-dwelling,

145

Handbill which was circulated in St Mary Cray

WARNING

ST MARY CRAY HAS THE HIGHEST STATISTICS FOR CRIMINAL DAMAGE, VANDALISM, AND CAR THEFT IN THE UNITED KINGDOM. THESE ACTS ARE COMMITTED BY A CERTAIN SECTION OF THE COMMUNITY KNOWN LOCALLY AS "PIKEY'S", THESE PEOPLE ARE WITHOUT ANY MORAL VALUES, ADULTS OR CHILDREN.

THEY HAVE NO CONSIDERATION OTHER THAN TO STEAL, DAMAGE, & VANDALISE. BEING OF EXCEPTIONALLY LOW MENTALITY THIS IS DONE SOLELY WITHOUT MOTIVE.

MOST OF THESE PEOPLE LIVE IN THE:

STAR LANE - HEARNS RISE - BARNFIELD ROAD - MAIDSTONE ROAD AREA'S OF THIS DISTRICT, AND ON THE NEW "RIVERBIRDS ESTATE".

THEY ARE SUPPORTED BY THE LOCAL LABOUR PARTY AND IT'S COUNCILLORS WHO HAVE AN OFFICE FOR THEIR WELFARE AT 13/15 HIGH STREET, ST MARY CRAY.

THE LAW ABIDING RESIDENTS OF THIS AREA HAVE ENDURED YEARS OF CONSTANT HARASSMENT FROM THIS MORONIC ELEMENT WITH NO SATISFACTORY RESPONSE FROM THE AUTHORITIES, POLICE, COUNCILLORS OF ALL POLITICAL PARTIES, YET WE PAY FOR ALL THE BENEFITS THIS ELEMENT RECEIVE.

ARE YOU GOING TO ALLOW THESE SCUM TO CONTINUE THEIR ACTIONS,

WE ARE NOT.

on the other hand, can absorb a lot of money and time; there is a much larger space to heat and fill with furniture and there is rent, council tax and bills for insurance, gas and electricity to pay. The economy of nomadic caravan-dwelling is almost a hand-to-mouth one as all purchases, whether a cylinder of gas, shopping for food or spares for the motor are immediate cash transactions. Bank accounts are for literate people whose domestic financial arrangements are dictated by the regularity and predictability of their lifestyle and salaries. Once in a house forward financial planning and budgeting becomes necessary and time is taken up by the need to have a permanent waged job in order to ensure the necessary continuity of income.

When this happens and dad is out at work all day, he no longer has his son by his side. The family thus spends even less time together and another link is broken in the generational chain. Instead, the children go to school because, once housed, there is no longer any practical difficulty in being able to attend and, now that they have a permanent address, someone will soon be knocking on the door if they don't. All parents naturally feel pangs of separation when their children are first sent to school: they have hitherto been solely responsible for their child's upbringing and have had a twenty-four-hour-a-day relationship with them. Giving them over to teachers can make any parent feel as if they have partially lost their child to the system. This feeling is exacerbated when Gypsy Travellers first hand their children into the care of a school peopled with teachers from another culture. Once in school the child will almost certainly be in a minority, or there may not be any other Travellers there at all.

> I went to primary school quite a bit but even then I used to get a lot of aggravation and, looking back on it now, I don't think it could have been quite so much the kids as what the parents had said to them. When you're a six-year-old and you're in a class and they're doing about different people and that stuff and the kids say, 'Oh, she's a Gypsy, she must live in one of those wagons,' that sort of thing. It wasn't too bad, you didn't notice it quite as much then. It was more at secondary school when trouble started because I was getting older myself and obviously as you're getting older you're becoming more aware yourself about things as well. I got a lot of aggravation in general from other people because, being a local family and being quite a big family, you couldn't — well I didn't want to deny who I was — but you couldn't get out of the fact of who you were and what you were. So that was a big problem, a lot of racial prejudice at school. You get all the thing, 'you dirty Gypsy' and that sort of thing, notes being passed round the class, teachers as bad, not doing anything about it, just turning a blind eye to it, so it didn't bother me not going in the end.
>
> Delaine leBas

> There is a lot that's ashamed to be Travellers today. It's because of the aggravation that they get through the schools and the children. It's like

Delaine and Damien leBas

*my children down the school now, I got one picked on all the time down
there, he's getting called this and he's getting called that. If there's anything going on in the school its 'Danny this' and Danny that', Danny's
done this', 'Danny's been fighting'. It's because of who he is and I don't
think it's right. I think they should be treated as equal, but they should
know that they have a different upbringing, which has a part in this.*

Sarah Hilden

Bit by bit the old Traveller ways are eroded and the Gypsy
inevitably moves step by step towards living the life of the
Gorjer. Gypsy culture was created and sustained by life on the
road and its customs, language, manners and organisation have
evolved to serve that way of life. It was when they pulled up on
a farm for picking or at one of the many horse fairs held annu-
ally across the country that Travellers renewed old friendships
and strengthened family bonds. These were times when gossip

Cherry picking, Pembury, 1992

and news were currency and there was homemade entertainment in the pubs or around the fires at night. The creative expression of the culture through the media of dance, music, song and storytelling is important, for these folk arts are essentially participatory and serve to bring people together, helping to strengthen the bonds between them. Today's entertainment is created and delivered by distant and aggressive media factories to passive recipients, their outpourings conforming to the new norms of the global fashion and pop music industries. Inevitably, the old inclusive and participatory traditions wither and, with their demise, the oral culture and use of the old language also decline.

> We're like a bridge and you cross over from the old to the new. Whereas
> life used to involve sitting round the fire and all the old ones would talk
> and tell you about their experiences and different things, the television

On Polhill, 1988

really has killed a lot of that because it kills the art of conversation. So therefore a lot of what we should have learnt from the last generation we've missed out on because where they would be outdoors telling each other stories, they don't do that any more, it's 'shh, be quiet, Coronation Street's on'. So the influence of what you should learn from the old ones is just disappearing.

Delaine's Mum

When I was younger we used to have television and used to watch cartoons, but I would much rather have gone out and listened to my grandad because he used to go on about the really old times — stories that you would never hear about, and we would sit down there for hours and hours on end just listening to him. We didn't care about all the technology, televisions and toys and playing with them, we just wanted to listen to him all the time, you know, I really miss that. I really miss the old things that he used to go on about and the old remedies. You get all like the aromatherapy stuff that's come out now, all that Travellers used to do back in the olden days, they used to go and find that up hedgerows. I wish that my grandad had had the education to write down everything about that so I could take it on to my generation and the next generation on from me. I wish that I could just go back there and say, 'come on, write it all down so we can take it on'. You never forget about that. That's one thing I used to miss and I really miss now. Now that my grandad's dead, I miss him telling me all the stories and all the things he used to go on about because they were so interesting. It was real life, it was about real life.

Sarah Hilden

You don't see people like you used to. When you was travelling around in caravans, you always met someone, either relations, distant relations or strangers. You sat round the fire and had a good talk. See, you could learn off the old ones, they used to educate us, tell us where we was going right and where we was going wrong. You was more happy, you see. Now, you don't see hardly anyone who you know. Romanies, they're not so together like the old people were, they don't knit together. You see, they used to knit together, the old Gypsies, they used to help one another, but it's the young generation, they weren't brought up like we were, not the old ones. You see, we got our own language, I can speak proper Romany, but if you talk to them in Romany, they wouldn't understand, they never had no interest in it.

Mark Hilden

Pembury, 1992

If I start talking in the Travellers' language, the biggest half of the
words, they don't know what I'm on about, they don't understand. The
main reason is why, is because all the Travellers is not based together, not
like it was years ago. If there was a crowd of them staying together,
well, one kid's picked it up off another, you know from what the parents
have learnt them, but where Gypsy kids have been parted up, the
language is just dying out. You get a bloke today in his forties, he would
know about the language, but if you get the kids today, the Gypsy kids
even to they're fifteen, I don't think they would know, only just a little
of the Gypsy language.

Bill Smith

Retaining the language in a world that preaches conformity
and homogenisation is difficult and now that their children
increasingly grow up amongst non-Travellers and attend
schools where the teachers disapprove of 'slang' and dialect,
there is less motivation to perpetuate and use Romanes. The
systematic destruction of the nomadic lifestyle has inevitably
had a considerable impact on the culture and communal identity of Gypsy Travellers. In spite of the hardships of the road, at
least the sense of being a Gypsy was maintained, but once
sedentary and deprived of those cultural touchstones, what is
there left to defend?

If you ask any of my three children what they are, they would say, 'we
are Traveller children'. They know what they are but they haven't been
brought up with Travellers, they can do all the talking but they haven't
been brought up as travelling children. I mean, they are completely different from me. When I was eleven or twelve, all we knew was playing
outside the trailer, not going nowhere and if you did it would be the
pictures with my mother, that was our weekly outing. But today, they
scream and cry for toys if you take them to the market or shops, they
want whatever they see and for eleven- and twelve-year-olds all they
know is a mirror, make up and hair spray. We didn't know any of that
when we were young, we were still in the wood playing camps when we
was their ages. Toys don't mean nothing to them today. Rolling skates
and two-wheeled ones and all that sort of thing, computers up there, a
five-minute wonder, mountain bikes. I had an old bike off a dump and I
thought the world of it, that was my new bike to me, I didn't care
where it came from. I got it off Harrietsham dump. I loved that old
bike, I played on that and looked after it. I used to have a dear little
dolly, or sometimes my mum used to make an old doll up in the fields,
an old sauce bottle with a teat on it and we'd play hours. But you take
my children out in a field and they cry all day, they're dry or they want

Sandwich bar, Biggin Hill, 2001

*an ice cream or they don't want to go here, or they don't want to go
there. It's just different today, I think, the children have been brought up
differently.*

Kay Smith

In 1983 John Wells, MP for Maidstone, was still perpetuating
the negative and defamatory views about Gypsies that he had
first voiced in the House of Commons twenty years previously.
During a debate on crime on 7 February 1983 he said, 'unless
we can break the vicious circle of Gypsy children not attending
schools and breeding, I am afraid frequently below the age of
consent, they will perpetuate the cycle of non-school attenders

East Sussex County Council

NO CARAVANNING

OR CAMPING

OR FILTHY PIKIES

A Sussex lay by, 1989

and petty criminals. All too often, offenders, not only Gipsies but other modest offenders who are broke, are fined. The fine is then paid by the social security system. You, Mr Deputy Speaker, and I, the Minister and the Shadow Minister and the rest of us pay the fine.'

Mr Wells made a number of assumptions in his speech – that Gypsy children frequently 'breed' below the age of sixteen, that they are petty criminals and live on social security. In the same year this kind of racially stereotyped prejudice was challenged when a case was brought under the 1976 Race Relations Act, in Mandla v Lee (I 983) IRLR 209. The House of Lords decided that for a group to constitute an 'ethnic group' for the purposes of the Act it must regard itself, and be regarded by others, as a distinct community by virtue of possessing a number of characteristics. These included having a long shared history, its own cultural traditions, a common geographical origin, literature, language and religion as well as being a minority within a dominant community. It was considered that the Gypsies fulfilled the criteria, and this acceptance of them as an ethnic minority was further reinforced by a test case brought to the Court of Appeal by the Commission for Racial Equality in July 1988. In the leading judgement Lord Justice Nicholls concluded that, 'Gypsies are an identifiable group of persons defined by reference to ethnic origins within the

Mark Hilden cherry
picking, 1987 (SE)

Pub in Medway Towns, 2001

meaning of the [Race Relations] Act.' The court found that the term 'Traveller' encompassed both Gypsies and other caravan dwellers and that a 'No Travellers' notice in a public house was, therefore, indirectly discriminatory. Indirect discrimination is illegal under the Race Relations Act 1976. The ruling made little difference in practice and although clearly against the law such notices are still to be seen in pub windows.

Racial prejudice takes many forms. Although overt discrimination may not always be evident, it is the small, everyday incidents or comments that continuously reinforce the barriers that Gorjer society erects against the Gypsy. These may no longer be the physical restrictions of ditches and banks but they still have a cumulative effect and remain a source of corrosive and incessant irritation.

Although Gypsy Travellers are legally recognised as a distinct ethnic group, an assumption of criminality is still perpetuated by politicians and others in authority despite the fact that such views are by definition racially prejudiced. Neither has being recognised as a distinct ethnic group particularly helped in terms of education or other publicly funded cultural provision. Although schools and libraries, for instance, must have a multicultural agenda, the Romany, Gypsy or Traveller is rarely included in the curriculum nor are allowances generally made for the fact that they have traditionally led a very different lifestyle.

*All they see in a Gypsy is little wagons and horses. I don't think they
actually think there's any more to it than that. I don't think they've got
any understanding that the Travellers' whole lifestyle is completely different to other people, the way they do things in their home, the way
they bring their children up, all the unwritten rules that there are, and I
think it's because of all these misconceptions that people have got about
them, that's why it's difficult for them to know how to approach you,
in a way. I don't think that when Traveller children go to school the way
they go about things is understood and there's a lot of different aspects
of their life that they could encourage them with. They just want to
pigeonhole Travellers and as long as they fit into that, like fitting a
square peg into a round hole, then that's okay. They don't want people to
be different. I thought the whole idea of learning was to able to question
things and to try and understand things properly from that point of
view, but it just seems that they want to tell people something and that's
it. They don't want to go any further than that, they don't want to
explore it in any other way or go round it in a different way. They just
want to ram something into your head and that's it. It's like if you
don't go to school and you don't wear school uniform or you've got your
ears pierced, or your parents won't let you do this, that or the other,
you're wrong for that and you should be doing what everyone else is
doing rather than being able to be different.*

Delaine leBas

Sarah (Opposite)

This inability to accommodate difference obviously results in
difficulties when Travellers enter the formal education system.
Traditionally, Traveller culture is largely spontaneous and
unplanned, routine being anathema to the freewheeling spirit.
This outlook on life does not sit easily with the punctuality and
regularity demanded by the education system. For previous
generations of Travellers, schooling was not something that
possessed value: all the skills necessary for a life on the road
were learned through being a valued member of the family,
regardless of age. Schooling is therefore entered into with trep-
idation.

*I think they're afraid of going into school or college and they don't
think they can cope with it because they've come from that background.
They don't think that their minds can cope with getting a better education, reading books and going into it more. But I think they shouldn't
be afraid of that. I mean, we can stand up for our rights more if we have
a better education. Back in the old days they couldn't stand up for their
rights because they didn't really know about the law and writing letters
and getting a better education through life. When I was little I wasn't*

159

Derby Day,
Epsom, 1988

brought up in the Gorjer's way. We were still travelling around but in
my teenager years we settled down and I've gone to school. But you never
forget about it, nor does anyone else. People can always point you out, it
doesn't matter how much you dress yourself up and how posh you get,
you can never, never, be like anyone else. You will always be a Gypsy and
you'll never get rid of that no matter how hard you try. People ever since
I've been going to school they still say, 'oh you dirty old Gypsy,' and all
this and you never forget who you are.

Sarah Hilding

Thus the problems continue even after leaving travelling
behind and adopting the sedentary lifestyle that those in
authority demanded. The process of settlement continued
relentlessly throughout the Seventies and Eighties, but some of
those who moved into houses still felt that they needed an
escape route, a reassurance that the transition into bricks and
mortar was not necessarily permanent or irreversible.

I know Travellers today who are in houses and they still buy caravans
and they pull in the garden. They've got to stay there because they've got
nowhere else to go. I mean, the council's put them in the house and as
far as the council knows, they're living in the house. Then the council
men come along to collect the rent or whatever and turn around and say,
'Oh you've got a caravan,' and they say, 'Oh yeah, we use that to go on

holiday.' But little do the council know, the Gypsies still use them to
sleep in at night when they've got them in the garden. If they want to
move, they turn around and pay the month's rent and they still travel.

Bill Smith

Although the process of becoming sedentary didn't happen
overnight, in comparison with the long history of nomadism it
had been a rapid process. Many older Travellers are now of the
opinion that the time will eventually come when there will be
no Gypsies at all. For them it was the travelling life that defined
them as 'real Romanies' and, once settled, they believe that the
culture that evolved and was sustained through movement will
inevitably wither. Only time will tell if they are right, but
moving into a house doesn't mean that the Gypsy suddenly
becomes a Gorjer. Traveller culture is liquid and by flowing
around fixed obstacles it moves on but retains its integrity and
structure. Most of the younger generation of Gypsies have
never followed a travelling life but still retain an acute sense of
cultural identity.

> There's a lot of Travellers who've lived in houses for quite a few years
> anyway. They don't seem to have lost anything in that. Like there are
> certain things they've got in their house, they've still got the way that
> they carry on on a day-to-day basis. They will have certain things they
> like that are peculiar just to them. A big part of it is the language and
> to a certain extent if you start losing too much of that, you can start
> losing other things as well. So, myself, we are trying to keep some of that
> going because I think it's important, it's just part of the whole thing. So
> if you can keep all the parts that are still here now going, then that
> should be enough to sustain it, really, because it seems to have sustained
> it for this long.

Delaine leBas

> They say you can pick a Traveller's house out. I mean, we have got a few
> horses' heads outside and a few frilly curtains up and a few plates in the
> windows. Like you get next door, his house was dead the same as mine.
> I've knocked the walls through, it's a wonder it's standing up really.
> We've knocked about three or four different walls out in here. But a lot
> of people coming in here say it reminds them more of a trailer than a
> house, so I suppose, yeah, we do try and make the houses look more like
> trailers inside. And I think to go back in a trailer now with no water, no
> electric and all that I'd most probably miss the house, deep down. I'm
> used to running the bath, getting up in the morning and switching that
> gas fire on. Not in a trailer, you've got to go out there and get the wood

Mrs Smith, Maidstone

and the coal, light the fires and everything else, go and get a churn of water. I don't think I could do the trailer, roaming round the roads again.

Kay Smith

I think you shouldn't forget who you really are because if you forget who you are, then you become nothing in the end. You should always remember your tradition, you know, even though things are changing, the world's changing and everything. You shouldn't forget that because you forget about your race, you forget all the things and then it all gets buried and then you get buried with it. Travellers today, they are ashamed of who they are because the government's put them down so much and said, 'Oh you dirty old Gypsies,' and everything like this, it's put them down. They want to be the Gorjer now, they don't want to be the Traveller any more because they're ashamed of that. They say, 'Oh no, don't say that I'm that, don't say that I'm a Gypsy and everything like that. No, I'm a Gorjer now because I live in a house.' They try to forget their past and forget who they are. I know people who do that, I won't mention their names but I do know people who do that. I don't think you should forget who you are because inside you're forgetting yourself. If you forget about your past life, then who are you in the end?

Sarah Hilding

It's important that what you've come from is what you are and to me everything that's a part of my past will be a part of my future because, without any sort of a past, I don't think you've got any present and you haven't got anything to build on. It's like trying to build a house on sand — if you haven't got any foundations, it's just going to fall over. I think that's all part of the whole thing. You can look back, but you can use looking back to look forward, rather than just seeing it in a negative way, that that's all gone and there's nothing you can do. But I think there are things you can do, ways you can go about things.

Delaine leBas

(Opposite) Reuben and his family, Green Street Green

Mushi

You cannot travel in this society. This society says, 'You cannot live an itinerant way of life.' Now, I think that as a Traveller I can identify other ways of travelling. I can identify other itinerancies. Where are Travellers going? Well, they are going anywhere and everywhere, but without change you're going nowhere, you're actually staying exactly where you are. That's the anathema to a Traveller way of life, to stay exactly where you are, you can travel in your mind, you can be a little more transient. I hope that what transient ways of thinking can bring to society, if that's not too grand a word, is the idea that everything moves. If it stays still then it stagnates. You see, Gypsies can't stay where they are. If they stay where they are, then they're not a Gypsy. You can start to say, not 'where I've been or where I am', and moan about that, but 'where I want to go', and why I want to go there and the romance and the beauty and joy of what's around the next corner. That's what really, at the end of the day, created Travellers, it wasn't something in your blood — we'll find a Traveller gene and we'll zap it so we won't have to travel anymore. No, it's not that, it's a curiosity, a burning curiosity to know what's over there. I know what's behind me, I have a very good idea of where I actually am, but what I'm really, really interested in is what's over there. That's what I would want to stay dear to, not my caravan, but caravans in the mystical sense of the word, the caravans of the mind.

Brian Belton

(next page) On Polhill